D0502970

BASIC AND ADVANCED
LIGHT PLANE MAINTENANCE

Rules and Inspections

The Light Plane Maintenance Library
Volume Six

BASIC AND ADVANCED
LIGHT PLANE MAINTENANCE

Rules and Inspections

By the Editors of *Light Plane*
Maintenance Magazine

Belvoir Publications, Inc.
Riverside, Connecticut

ISBN: 0-9615196-1-4

Please Note: The information appearing in this publication is presented for educational purposes only. In no case shall the publisher be held responsible for any use readers may choose to make (or not to make) of this information. Readers are hereby advised that Federal Aviation Regulation 91.163(a) places primary responsibility for ensuring the airworthy condition of any aircraft on the aircraft owner or operator. Any person who performs inspections, alterations, and/or repairs on any aircraft does so entirely at his or her own risk.

Contents

Preface

This book is part of The Light Plane Maintenance Library, a series of guides intended to provide information about aircraft and aircraft maintenance to pilots and owners. These volumes have been created to enable our readers to achieve better performance, economy, and enjoyment from their aircraft.

The materials in these pages have been drawn from articles published over several years in *Light Plane Maintenance* Magazine, the most highly respected general aviation journal of its kind.

Rules and Inspections is a key volume in the Light Plane Maintenance Library, for it addresses questions that every aircraft owner faces from when he first obtains his aircraft, through coping with annual inspections and other examinations, to the point when he sells it. This book discusses the Federal Aviation Administration's regulations regarding owner-performed maintenance, various kinds of inspection, basic points about aircraft hardware, and the principles of rigging maintenance.

Every year, many aircraft purchasers and owners suffer unnecessary difficulties and expense because they are unfamiliar with measures they can take to inspect airplanes when considering them for purchase, new or used. Similarly, many owners do not realize that by performing certain inspections and buying at least some parts on their own, they can reduce the costs of annual inspections. Such owners often neglect to seek the best shop to perform their annuals and therefore waste money and even risk post-inspection mechanical failure.

The costs of maintaining an aircraft are high, usually much higher than they need be. By performing legal maintenance himself or herself—including observing a well-disciplined program of inspection between annuals—an owner can save on shop labor and parts costs while establishing a healthy familiarity with the aircraft's systems and condition.

To do that, he must have a fundamental knowledge of aircraft

hardware, a subject more easily grasped than the average owner suspects.

How an aircraft is rigged determines how efficiently and comfortably it flies, yet it often is neglected by owners and professional mechanics. From manufacture through operation, aircraft rigging can go bad and that can lead to increased fuel costs and pilot discomfort, not to mention, in extreme cases, flight hazards.

Some of the lessons in this book are presented through case-history narratives. We believe that participating in the experiences of those who have the technical expertise to understand those experiences can be enlightening for maintenance neophytes as well as more seasoned practitioners. When we present such experiences, we do so in the confidence that these examples will be relevant to the readers' needs. The articles that make up this book were written with the reader's interest foremost in mind, and that spirit has been retained in the preparation of the Light Plane Maintenance Library.

Because *LPM* has a strong personal concern for the flying welfare of general aviation pilots, we take some ''political'' stands regarding FAA regulations and requirements and the practices of some fixed-base operators and mechanics. General aviation is nowhere near perfect, and we hope that our readers will benefit from a recognition that there may be better ways of doing things than are now the law or common practice.

Finally, the danger of error through obsolescence has discouraged us from quoting prices and costs and referring to individual shops or firms. For current information on costs and services, we recommend that the reader consult *Light Plane Maintenance* Magazine.

Riverside, Connecticut
April 1987

Part I
LEGALITIES

Chapter 1

PILOT-PERFORMED MAINTENANCE

The rules governing pilot-performed (non-A&P) maintenance are among the most widely misunderstood Federal Aviation Regulations on the books. And for good reason. They very often don't make sense.

Most of us, at one time or another, have changed an airplane's oil filter, believing this to be a "preventive maintenance" procedure. In actual fact, it is not permitted under any existing regulation.

Ask any FAA official whether you (as a pilot/owner, with neither an A nor a P mechanic's rating) may legally disassemble your plane's brakes—and the answer you'll get will almost certainly be "no." Yet, the FARs say you *can* change a tire yourself—and in the process of changing a main-gear tire, you *must* disassemble the brake at the wheel. (Otherwise, you could not remove the wheel from the axle.)

Present regulations forbid you from replacing your plane's windshield yourself—although you may legally replace side windows.

You may legally replace pre-fabricated fuel lines yourself. You may not replace pre-fabbed *brake* lines.

You may troubleshoot and repair defects in landing light circuits. You may *not* troubleshoot or repair defects in cockpit light circuits, or rotating beacon circuits.

Want to replace a worn generator belt? Sorry, present FARs forbid it. You'll have to find a mechanic to help you. (Not just to *help* you, but to sign the work off in your engine or airframe logbook, too.)

Only a licensed mechanic can take nicks out of a prop.

And so it goes. Nobody, it seems, has a clear idea of exactly what actually constitutes 100-percent-legal pilot-performed maintenance—including the FAA's maintenance inspectors. *Even the FAA* lacks a clear, consistent policy regarding "preventive maintenance."

What (if anything), then, *can* a pilot legally do to his or her plane in the way of routine maintenance? How thin is the legal ice upon which pilot-mechanics stand? What are the chances that a pilot—if caught doing illegal preventive maintenance (dressing out a prop blade, for instance)—would lose his license *or his plane*? To find the answers to these and other questions, we went to 800 Independence Avenue, S.W., in Washington, D.C.—FAA headquarters—where we spent approximately eight hours talking with ten individuals over a three-day period. We came away from our talks with a much better understanding of how the regulatory process (and FAA psychology) works, what the existing regulations mean—and why the regulations need to be changed.

700,000-plus Licensed Mechanics

The fact that pilots are legally entitled to perform at least *some* forms of mechanical work is made clear by FAR 43.3(h), which states: "The holder of a pilot certificate issued under Part 61 may perform preventive maintenance on any aircraft owned or operated by him that is not used in air carrier service." In other words, a pilot's certificate—*any* pilot's certificate—constitutes not only a license to fly but a license to perform *limited maintenance* ("preventive maintenance," in aeronautical parlance).

The implications of this are worth pondering for a moment. FAR 43.3(h) renders every pilot in the U.S. a potential practitioner of preventive maintenance. Another way of looking at this is that there are some more than 700,000 *licensed aircraft mechanics in the U.S. today*. These "mechanics" are limited to performing only *preventive* maintenance, but preventive maintenance already accounts (in theory, if not actual practice) for about 25 percent of *all* maintenance, and there is no reason why it could not be made to encompass 50 percent of all maintenance, if pilots would simply take more of an interest in *prevention* as a maintenance strategy, as opposed to corrective fence-mending, which is the dominant strategy now.

Note that FAR 43.3(h) allows you to perform preventive maintenance on any aircraft *owned or operated* by you. It does not allow you to work on anyone else's plane.

The big question, of course, is: What constitutes "preventive maintenance"? Here, we begin to enter legal limbo. FAR Part 1 defines preventive maintenance as "simple or minor preservation operations and the replacement of small standard parts not involving complex assembly operations.''

Obviously, that definition covers a lot of ground. Some idea of just how much territory it covers can be gained from Appendix A of FAR Part 43, which lists 27 examples of types of work that the FAA considers preventive maintenance for airplanes. According to Appendix A, ''work of the following type'' is preventive maintenance:

[1] Removal, installation, and repair of landing gear tires.

[2] Replacing elastic shock absorber cords on landing gear.

[3] Servicing landing gear shock struts by adding oil, air, or both.

[4] Servicing landing gear wheel bearings, such as cleaning and greasing.

[5] Replacing defective safety wiring or cotter keys.

[6] Lubrication not requiring disassembly other than removal of nonstructural items such as cover plates, cowlings, and fairings.

[7] Making simple fabric patches not requiring rib stitching or the removal of structural parts or control surfaces.

Beneath the covers of your plane are surprisingly plentiful opportunities for keeping the aircraft fit by doing the work yourself.

[8] Replenishing hydraulic fluid in the hydraulic reservoir.

[9] Refinishing decorative coating of fuselage, wings, tail group surfaces (excluding balanced control surfaces), fairings, cowling, landing gear, cabin, or cockpit interior when removal or disassembly of any primary structure or operating system is not required.

[10] Applying preservative or protective material to components where no disassembly of any primary structure or operating system is involved and where such coating is not prohibited or is not contrary to good practices.

[11] Repairing upholstery and decorative furnishings of the cabin or cockpit interior when the repairing does not require disassembly of any primary structure or operating system or interfere with an operating system or affect the primary structure of the aircraft.

[12] Making small simple repairs to fairings, nonstructural cover plates, cowlings, and small patches and reinforcements not changing the contour so as to interfere with proper airflow.

[13] Replacing side windows where that work does not interfere with the structure or any operating system such as controls, electrical equipment, etc.

[14] Replacing safety belts.

[15] Replacing seats or seat parts with replacement parts approved for the aircraft, not involving disassembly of any primary structure or operating system.

[16] Troubleshooting and repairing broken circuits in landing light wiring circuits.

[17] Replacing bulbs, reflectors, and lenses of position and landing lights.

[18] Replacing wheels and skis where no weight and balance computation is involved.

[19] Replacing any cowling not requiring removal of the propeller or disconnection of flight controls.

[20] Replacing or cleaning spark plugs and setting of spark plug gap clearance.

[21] Replacing any hose connection except hydraulic connection.

[22] Replacing prefabricated fuel lines.

[23] Cleaning fuel and oil strainers.

[24] Replacing batteries and checking fluid level and specific-gravity.

Not only for the aircraft owner but for FAA representatives, the twists and tangles of the FARs that govern preventive maintenance can be more convoluted than the innards of an aircraft.

[25] Removing and installing glider wings and tail surfaces that are specifically designed for quick removal and installation and when such removal and installation can be accomplished by the pilot.

[26] Replacement or adjustment of nonstructural standard fasteners incidental to operations.

[27] The installation of anti-misfueling devices to reduce the diameter of fuel tank filler openings, provided the specific device has been made a part of the aircraft type certificate data by the aircraft manufacturer, the aircraft manufacturer has provided FAA-approved instructions for installation of the specific device, and installation does not involve the disassembly of the existing tank filler opening.

All of the above types of work are considered ''preventive maintenance'' by the FAA. Does this mean that *only* the 27 types of work listed qualify as pilot-performable tasks? Is Appendix A of Part 43 the *final word* on what pilots may and may not do to their planes? It depends on whom inside the FAA you ask. If you ask your local GADO (General Aviation District Office) officials, you'll probably be told that Appendix A is merely a *guideline* for determining what constitutes preventive maintenance, that it is *not* an exhaustive callout of what pilots can and cannot do. (When we called the Charlotte, North Carolina GADO and asked the chief maintenance people whether the list of items in Appendix A was exhaustive, we were told that not only was it *not* an exhaustive list, but some of the items on it would not qualify as ''preventive maintenance'' for some types of aircraft. For example, we were told that if we owned a Learjet, replacement of prefabricated fuel lines would not be considered preventive maintenance, Appendix A notwithstanding.)

The people at FAA headquarters in Washington have a slightly different view: The official headquarters interpretation of Appendix A is that it does, in fact, constitute an exhaustive list of preventive maintenance procedures. From an enforcement standpoint, Appendix A of Part 43 is etched in stone. A pilot can be nailed for attempting any kind of work not listed therein—unless the pilot is working under a mechanic's tutelage.

The rulemakers in Washington concede that some types of work not mentioned in Appendix A probably should be. Robert Blacker and Wayne Sprague of the FAA's Office of Airworthiness are quick to point out that air and oil filter servicing, vacuum filter replacement, and brake puck installation (to name but a few examples) are all jobs that any conscientious owner/pilot can safely carry out, jobs that probably ought to be listed in Appendix A of Part 43. ''I don't doubt that the average plane owner can do these things, and do them right,'' Sprague explains. ''Unfortunately, if I had to sit down and write out a complete list of everything a person could reasonably be expected to do to his or her own plane in the name of 'preventive maintenance,' the rule book would be a mile thick. Where do you draw the line?''

Granted, the question of where to draw the line is not an easy one. (Nobody ever said rulemaking would be easy.) We think the ''line'' ought to be drawn a little bit further down the football field than it now is.

Chapter 2

SUPERVISION
AND STANDARDS

Thus far, we've talked only about the kinds of work a pilot can perform unsupervised and unassisted. It turns out that with a little help from a licensed A and/or P mechanic, a pilot can do a great deal more than just the things listed above. In fact, if he or she is working

under the supervision of a mechanic, a pilot can do nearly anything, including engine overhauls.

WORK/SUPERVISION GUIDELINES

FAR Part 43.3(d) states something worth reading closely:

"A person working under the supervision of a holder of a mechanic or repairman certificate may perform the maintenance, preventive maintenance, and alterations that his supervisor is authorized to perform, if the supervisor personally observes the work being done properly and if the supervisor is readily available, in person, for consultation. However, this paragraph does not authorize the performance of any inspection required by Part 91 or Part 125 of this chapter or any inspection performed after a major repair or alteration."

This is the regulation that makes it legal for engine overhaul shops to hire non-A&P-rated personnel to assemble engines. It's also the rule that makes it possible for FBOs short on shop help to hire "mechanic's assistants" fresh off the street.

The key thing to note regarding FAR 43.3(d) is that the supervising mechanic (or repairman) not only must observe the work being done to the extent necessary to ensure a good job, but he must also be available _in person_ for consultation. In other words, if a roving FAA inspector catches you replacing your plane's alternator by yourself and asks where your mechanic is, and you say, "He's out to lunch right now, but he'll be back in a couple hours to check my work," you're likely to be written up.

If FAR 43.3(d) sounds like a pretty good deal, it is. The only catch is that while you can indeed do the work yourself (whether it involves replacing an alternator or hanging a new engine), you _cannot_ legally return the plane to service when you're done. Only your mechanic can do this, and _he_ can do it only if a log entry is made giving a description of the work, the date of completion, the name(s) of the person(s) performing the work, and the signature—and certificate number—of the person approving the aircraft for return to service. (All of this is spelled out in FAR 43.5.) In other words, a mechanic (or repairman) must _sign off_ any non-preventive maintenance you do. It isn't enough just to have supervision. You also have to arrange for a logbook sign-off.

Furthermore, FAR 43.5 recently has been rewritten to require pilots to make log entries following *preventive* maintenance. Owner/pilots would in fact do well to keep the current version of Part 43.5 in mind:

No person may approve for return to service any aircraft, airframe, aircraft engine, propeller, or appliance, that has undergone maintenance, rebuilding, or alteration unless—

[a] The maintenance record entry required by Part 43.9 or Part 43.11, as appropriate, has been made;

[b] The repair or alteration form authorized by the Administrator has been executed in a manner prescribed by the Administrator; and

[c] If a repair or an alteration results in any change in the aircraft operating limitations or flight data contained in the approved flight manual, those operating limitations of flight data are appropriately revised and set forth as prescribed in Part 91.31.

Rules for Performance

The fact that pilots are allowed to perform certain types of work without supervision does not mean that the performance standards that apply to professional mechanics don't also apply to pilots. Actually, the same standards *do* apply. According to FAR 43.13(a):

"Each person maintaining or altering, or performing preventive maintenance, shall use methods, techniques, and practices acceptable to the Administrator. He shall use the tools, equipment, and test apparatus necessary to assure completion of the work in accordance with accepted industry practices. If special equipment or test apparatus is recommended by the manufacturer involved, he must use that equipment or apparatus or its equivalent acceptable to the Administrator."

The question of what constitutes "methods, techniques, and practices acceptable to the Administrator" has been answered in copious detail in two mammoth Advisory Circulars known as AC 43.13-1A("Acceptable Methods, Techniques, and Practices: Aircraft Inspection and Repair") and AC 43.13-2A ("Acceptable Methods, Techniques, and Practices: Aircraft Alterations"). These formidable documents, which comprise more than 400 pages in all (in their current editions), set forth acceptable practices relating to the repair and/or adjustment of just about every aircraft component or subcomponent you can imagine. These two books are considered the bibles of the industry. Certainly, anyone contemplating performing any type of maintenance on any aircraft, preventive or not, ought to consider AC 43.13-1A & 2A required reading. (Available from the Superintendent of Documents, Government Printing Office, Washington, DC 20402; ask for SN 050-011-00461-3 and 050-007-00407-9. Spell out the books' titles, too.)

In addition to prescribing the *methods* to be used in performing aircraft maintenance (including preventive maintenance), the FAA has a few noteworthy things to say about the *end results* that must be achieved by those methods. In particular, FAR 43.13(b) states:

"Each person maintaining or altering, or performing preventive maintenance, shall do that work in such a manner and use materials of such a quality, that the condition of the aircraft, airframe, aircraft engine, propeller, or appliance worked on will be at least equal to its original or properly altered condition (with regard to aerodynamic function, structural strength, resistance to vibration and deterioration, and other qualities affecting airworthiness)."

In other words, if you decide to clean and lubricate your plane's

In performing very simple or highly complex maintenance tasks, the owner is governed by a voluminous body of regulations setting forth what is "acceptable to the Administrator." Clarity and consistency are not always built into these rules.

wheel bearings, you must perform the work in such a way—and use cleaning solvents and bearing grease of such a quality—that the wheel bearings will (when you're done) be as good as new, or at least in as good a condition as they would be if a professional technician had done the work. Also, you would have to do the job using the same kinds of tools (wrenches, jacks, etc.) that a mechanic would use—and those tools, in turn, would have to be used in accordance with the recommendations

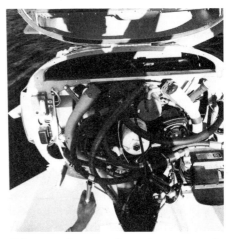

If the manufacturer of a part you are working on recommends using a particular tool, under the regs, you can be violated for using a different implement, however effective it may be.

given by the manufacturer (as well as by AC 43.13-1A & 2A).

Theory vs. Practice

Knowing what the regulations mean is one thing. Abiding by them is something else again. Despite a plane owner's best efforts, it is practically impossible to live within the letter of the law where maintenance is concerned. Technically speaking, based on the FAA headquarters interpretation of Part 43, any non-A&P-rated pilot who *services an air filter* without a logbook sign-off by a mechanic is violating the law.

Likewise, any pilot who files nicks out of his prop (or bleeds his brakes, or tightens his generator belt) without a mechanic's sign-off is violating the law.

Any pilot who performs *any* maintenance procedure *on a plane that is not his* (i.e., a rented or borrowed aircraft) is technically violating FAR 43.3(h).

In fact, technically speaking, if you use a 12-point deep socket to remove and install spark plugs—and if your plane is equipped with Champion plugs—you are violating FAR 43.13(a). Why? If special equipment is recommended by the manufacturer, says FAR

43.13(a), you must use it. Champion recommends the use of a 6-point deep socket for spark plug removal, rather than a 12-pointer.

Suffice to say, there probably isn't a pilot—or a mechanic—in the U.S. who hasn't violated (wittingly or un-) at least *some* sections of FAR Part 43. It's impossible not to.

What are your chances of actually being *written up* for violating the Federal Aviation Regulations pertaining to maintenance? Until now, they've been rather slim. FAA's Bob Blacker told us: "I don't know of a single enforcement action that's ever been taken against a plane owner for relining his own brakes, say, or changing his own oil filter." Most of the FAA's enforcement activities in the area of maintenance center around the big—and more recently, the small—air carriers. And even here, the violations usually must be repeated and/or flagrant for normal enforcement proceedings to be undertaken.

Even so, we do not find very palatable the idea that the FAA could—if it so chose—initiate enforcement proceedings against virtually any aircraft owner in the country, on the basis of alleged violations of FAR Part 43. The penalties for violating sections of the FARs are quite severe, ranging from fines of up to $1,000 per violation to suspension of aircraft airworthiness and/or registration certificates, to *outright seizure of the aircraft*. (See FAR 13.17, "Seizure of aircraft.") Frankly, we do not think it likely that the FAA would actually seize an aircraft merely because the owner had engaged in non-preventive maintenance activities without a mechanic's sign-off. But the FAA's policies *have* become increasingly punitive in nature of late, and enforcement activity is, without question, on the rise. In addition, everyone in Washington these days (it seems) is looking for new ways to increase revenues without increasing taxes; imposing more (and bigger) fines on rule-breakers is an attractive strategy in this regard.

We feel, on principle, that any law which renders the majority of people affected by it criminals is by definition a bad law. And we feel bad laws ought to be eliminated or rewritten, no matter how difficult the task. Appendix A, as it stands now, is a poorly written, narrowly conceived and largely outdated regulation. (We read in Appendix A about "fabric patches not requiring rib stitching," and yet we see nothing about air filters or oil filters.) Appendix A cries out for a top-to-bottom rewrite.

In summary: We see little sense in a law that says, on the one hand, that preventive maintenance consists of "simple or minor preservation operations and the replacement of small standard parts not involving complex assembly operations" and on the other hand, that preventive maintenance actually consists only of arbitrarily selected items listed in an appendix to Part 43. We see little sense in a law that says that a pilot can remove the wheels and wheel bearings from an airplane (disassembling the brakes in the process) but *cannot* replace a worn set of brake pucks.

We see little or no logic in not rewriting a bad regulation simply because it would be difficult to do so.

And finally, we fail to see any justification in the FAA's policy of doing nothing to broaden the maintenance prerogatives of more than 700,000 pilots at a time when a mechanic shortage of colossal proportions threatens general aviation.

Pilots and mechanics alike need a set of maintenance regulations we can live with. The present set represents a good first draft (for which the Civil Aeronautics Administration certainly ought to be commended). Time now to finish the job.

AIRCRAFT PARTS: WHICH ARE LEGAL?

The nature of aircraft parts, as defined by the regulations, can pose equally worrisome and confusing questions for owners who

Staying on the legal side regarding such parts as sun-visors is made possible by FAR 21.303. Various FARs govern various do-it-yourself applications.

wish to avoid both unnecessary expense and legal problems. For example, is it legitimate to replace the sun-visor in the window of your Bonanza with a visor of your own design? Do waxes and polishes—not to mention common lubricants like WD-40 and 3-in-1 Oil—have to be approved by the FAA? What about the Ford door handle in an out-of-production Piper? How can an owner be *sure* that a particular replacement part is legal for his or her airplane? Just what is it that makes an aircraft part an *aircraft* part?

We all know that things like tires, turn indicators, and ELTs are produced under Technical Standard Order (TSO) specifications and, as such, come with the FAA's blessing. But what about non-TSO items, such as that sun-visor or door handle?

Furthermore, would it be possible legally to fabricate one's own parts?

It may startle you to learn that nowhere in the Federal Aviation Regulations is there a reg stating "no person may install any part on an airplane unless it is FAA-approved." The only reg that even comes close is FAR 43.13 (which is well worth engraving on your toolbox lid and which we quote again for emphasis):

"Each person maintaining or altering, or performing preventive maintenance, shall use methods, techniques, and practices acceptable to the Administrator. He shall use the tools, equipment, and test apparatus necessary to assure completion of the work *in accordance with accepted industry practices.*" Furthermore: "Each person maintaining or altering, or performing preventive maintenance, shall do that work in such a manner and use materials of such a quality, that the condition of the aircraft, airframe, aircraft engine, propeller, or appliance worked on will be at least equal to its *original or properly altered condition.*" (Emphasis added.)

The concept of *type design* comes into play as well. Under FAR 21.31, "The type design consists of (a) the drawings and specifications necessary to show the configuration of the product concerned . . . (b) information on dimensions, materials, and processes necessary to define the structrual strength of the product; and (c) any other data necessary to allow, by comparison, the determination of the airworthiness and noise characteristics (where applicable) of later products of the same type." A *type certificate* applicable to the type designs entitles the holder (i.e., Cessna, Beech, etc.) to obtain airworthiness certificates and "obtain approval of replacement parts for that product'' (FAR 21.45). The validity of the airworthiness certificate hinges on adherence to the type design. So for example, if Cessna decides to include a Ford C7FF10300C alternator as part of an airplane's type design (which it has a right to do), then the arbitrary substitution—by you or your mechanic—of, say, a Delco alternator for the Ford P/N will have the effect of *invalidating the airworthiness certificate.* This in turn puts you at odds with FAR 91.203 (formerly 91.27), which requires U.S. civil aircraft to have a valid airworthiness certificate. Your insurance is probably no good at this point, also.

Technical Standard Orders (TSOs) are often thought of as governing the ''aircraftness'' of aircraft parts, but in fact TSOs are in most cases not mandatory standards—they merely outline *acceptable* performance standards for certain types of equipment. For example, a TSO exists for marker beacon receivers, but no one is required to comply with the TSO. Other TSOs are mandatory for air-carrier aircraft, but not for Part 91 aircraft (the VOR-receiver TSO is an example of this). Still other TSOs, such as the ones for transponders, combustion heaters, and turnbuckles, are mandatory across the board. For example, TSO C21a on turnbuckles says: ''Minimum performance standards are hereby established for special turnbuckle assemblies and/or safetying devices which are to be used on civil aircraft of the United States. New models of [these items] manufactured on or after July 1, 1958 shall meet the performance requirements as set forth in sections 3 and 4 of Military Specification MIL-T-5685A dated April 6, 1950 with the additional tests, when applicable, listed below.''

What TSOs Cover

Notice that TSOs are *performance* specifications (not manufacturing specifications per se). To market a part as TSO'd requires a TSO Authorization, which is granted after an FAA review of manufacturing and quality control standards.

Notice also that TSOs themselves are FARs. They are specific provisions of Part 21, Subpart O. (At one time, TSOs comprised Part 37 of the Federal Aviation Regulations, but Part 37 was revoked in 1980 after its relevant provisions were incorporated into Part 21. You can stump most mechanics with this.)

As even this partial list of TSOs indicates, TSOs cover a wide range of items:

Type of Equipment	TSO No.	Type of Equipment	TSO No.
Cargo smoke detectors	C1b	ADF receivers	C41c
Airspeed indicators	C2c	Temp. indicators (CHT)	C43a
Turn-and-bank	C3c	Fuel flowmeters	C44a
Attitude indicator	C4c	Manifold pressure gages	C45
Directional gyro	C5d	Pressure gages (fuel, oil)	C47
Gyro-stabilized compass	C6c	Audio amplifiers/panels	C50c
Magnetic compass	C7c	Flight directors	C52a
Rate of climb indicator	C8b	Engine hose assemblies	C53a
Autopilots	C9b	Fuel/oil quantity gages	C55
Barometric altimeter	C10b	Aircraft tires	C62b
Fire detectors	C11d	Weather radar	C63c
Life rafts	C12c	ATC transponders	C74c
Life preservers	C13d	Hydraulic hose assemblies	C75
Aircraft fabric, intermediate	C14a	Fuel drain valves	C76
Aircraft fabric, grade A	C15c	Flexible fuel cell materials	C80
Electric pitots	C16	Radar altimeters	C87
Fire-resistant materials	C17a	ELTs	C91
Portable fire extinguishers	C19b	Ground proximity alerters	C92b
Combustion heaters	C20	Lithium batteries	C97
Turnbuckles	C21a	Child restraint systems	C100
Safety belts	C22f	MLS receivers	C104
Wheels and brakes	C26b		
Position lights	C30b	[Note: To obtain copies of any of these
HF radios	C31c	TSOs, write: FAA, Office of Airwor-
Position light flashers	C33	thiness, Aircraft Engineering Division,
Marker beacon receivers	C35d	AWS-100, 800 Independence Ave.,
Seats and berths	C39a	S.W., Washington, DC 20591.]

Of course, TSOs don't cover everything. For instance, there is no TSO for piston rings. What makes a ring (or a locknut, or a flap-gap seal) ''approved'' or ''not approved''? Part 21 has the answer.

Subpart K of FAR Part 21 (''Approval of Materials, Parts, Processes, and Appliances'') states that ''except as provided in paragraph (b) of this section, no person may produce a modification or replacement part for sale for installation on a type-certficated product unless it is produced pursuant to a Parts Manufacturing Approval issued under this Subpart.''

Paragraph (b) of FAR 21.303 then lists the exceptions to the rule. ''This section does not apply to the following:

''1. Parts produced under a type or production certificate.

''2. Parts produced by an owner or operator for maintaining or altering his own product.

''3. Parts produced under an FAA Technical Standard Order.

''4. Standard parts (such as bolts and nuts) conforming to established industry or United States specifications.''

The Make-It-Yourself Exception

Let's take these items one by one. ''Parts produced under a type certificate'' obviously refers to things like ailerons, wings, and other components actually built by Cessna, Beech, Continental, Lycoming, etc. It also can cover a variety of smaller, vendor-made items (which must pass through the TC holder's Production Inspection System, as outlined in FAR 21.125), such as wheels, brakes, alternators, magnetos, etc.

Parts produced under a production certificate includes STC'd parts. (All holders of Supplemental Type Certificates who manufacture parts must do so under a production certificate per FAR 21, Subpart G.)

Item number two on the list is worth rereading. It allows owners and operators to *make parts themselves*, essentially without restric-

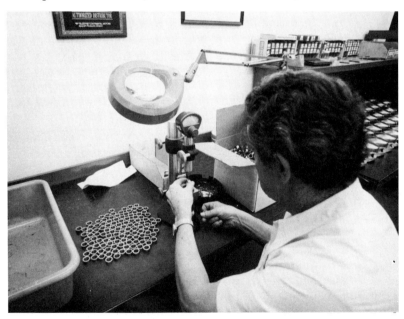

You can make your own bushings with the blessings of the Feds, as long as you have the proper materials, facilities, and QC documentation.

tions (although of course under FAR 43.13 you must ensure that your plane is returned to its "original or properly altered condition"). Got a bad bushing in the pinion end of your Bendix-type starter adapter? FAR 21.303(b)(2) allows you to machine your own replacement. You can make your own wing ribs if you want to. Just don't sell them to anyone else.

TSO'd parts qualify as FAA-approved, naturally. So, too, do *standard* parts conforming to established industry (SAE, ASTM, AMS, etc.) or United States (AN, NAS, Mil-Spec) specifications. What makes an AN4 bolt an aircraft bolt? Nothing, other than the fact that it is manufactured according to Air Force/Navy (AN) standards (which specify tensile strength, dimensions, thread type, and so on, for AN-type hardware).

Anything that *doesn't* fall into one of the above categories *must* be manufactured under a PMA (Parts Manufacturer Approval) in order to be sold as an "aircraft part." Subpart K of Part 21 spells out a variety of quality control and other requirements that must be met before a part can be produced under a PMA.

Some common examples of PMA parts are found in the engine-components aftermarket. FAA-PMA replacement parts include magneto coils (Aero Accessories, Electro-systems), piston rings (Superior, Precision), and oil filters (AC, Champion), among many others.

Vendor parts made for OEMs (original equipment manufacturers) often are not PMA approved. For example, the Rajay turbocharger on a Continental TSIO-360-FB carries a Continental part number and is approved for the engine under Continental's type certificate. Roto-Master (the manufacturer of the turbo) will not sell you a Rajay replacement for your Turbo Arrow, however, because the Roto-Master factory has no PMA. The approval falls strictly under Continental's umbrella.

Substitution Rules

Of course, the mere fact that a part exists and is TSO'd or PMA approved doesn't necessarily mean it is legal for use on your plane, if it wasn't there to begin with. Substitutions of parts, and the addition of parts not previously there to begin with, constitute changes in the airplane's type design and necessitate STC approval under FAR 21.113. No doubt an AiResearch turbo exists that will work on your engine, but unless the turbo is part of the Type Certificate Data Sheets for the airplane and engine, you'll negate your Airworthiness Certificate by putting the turbo on. Ditto for unapproved magnetos, alternators, or starter motors.

But can you replace your Bonanza's sun-visors with ones of your own design? You can, because FAR 21.303 allows you to make your own parts. Do waxes, polishes, and spray lubricants have to be FAA-approved? No. FAR 43.13 requires that maintenance be done in accordance with accepted industry practices, using "materials of such a quality that the condition of the aircraft, airframe, aircraft engine, propeller or appliance worked on will be at least equal to its original or properly altered condition." When you see an A&P spraying WD-40 on a piano hinge, he is doing so in accordance with accepted industry practices; you can do it too.

As for the out-of-production Piper door handle that you've discovered actually comes from a Ford Falcon (or whatever): This is a gray area. Without PMA approval, Ford can't legally sell aircraft parts. (The part's original approval came under Piper's TC umbrella—with all the incoming quality-control and other paperwork requirements that that implies.) On the other hand, if the part is truly identical, putting it on the plane won't violate the type design—in fact, it will return the aircraft to its original or properly altered condition. Since no FAR requires you to name sources for parts, give the names of manufacturers, or list actual part numbers in maintenance records, it is unlikely you would ever be called to task for putting the part on. *If* it's identical, that is. (Many non-aircraft parts—such as alternators and regulators—that *look* identical to "approved" parts *often turn out not to be.* Proceed with extreme caution.)

A final tip: Any part that can be removed between flights generally doesn't have to carry FAA approval. CFIIs who "install" non-PMA soap pads on gyro-instrument faces (and owners who attach timers and pencil-holders to the panel with Velcro) needn't fear FAA prosecution. Just be sure to un-install the goods before each annual inspection.

While the regulations that govern preventive maintenance contain convolutions that could drain a law firm skilled in major mergers, sound maintenance within the rules is possible and to the owner's advantage. An awareness of potential pitfalls, a lot of forethought, and a willingness to seek expert advice when confused can make the twists and turns of legality navigable.

In this as in all maintenance work, perserverance helps and neatness counts.

Part II
BASIC NUTS AND BOLTS

Chapter 3

THE PILOT'S TOOL KIT

This book is not intended to be a thriller—we leave that to the Deightons, Ludlums, Le Carres, and Ganns of this world. What is supposed to thrill you about light plane maintenance is the collection of benefits you will gain from learning how to work on your own aircraft, as far as the law will allow. Among these benefits are a sense of achievement, a glowing awareness of having saved expense, pride in having made your airplane more intimately "your own," and the general pleasure that comes with understanding the workings of airplanes and therefore the intricacies of flight. As they have become proficient at it, many people have even come to enjoy the work of maintenance for its own sake—they have become happy craftsmen. We don't promise that will happen, but don't be too sure that it won't. Accruing these benefits demands study and patience, however, especially when it comes to reading such dry stuff as discussions of aircraft hardware.

In his classic book, *Weekend Pilot*, Frank Kingston Smith aptly captured the essence of most pilots' distaste for dead reckoning when he observed that "navigation is spinach." Well, if navigation is spinach, then aircraft hardware (as a subject of study) must rank somewhere between turnip greens and kale. For while dead reckoning is at least *somewhat* palatable to most aviators, the subject of aircraft hardware, alas, is not.

Still, pilots who wish to become involved in performing their own minor maintenance should know something about the classification (and proper use) of AN, NAS, and MS hardware before taking wrench in hand. They should also have an idea of how best to perform such a basic and frequent job as safety-wiring. And, as we shall see in this chapter, they should know what tools and materials are a rock-bottom must for doing the work.

Quite simply, there is no point in trying to perform aircraft

A multi-bit screwdriver pays for itself. The hollow handle in the model shown above stores the bits, which are magnetic, to help retrieve screws.

maintenance (minor or not) without this fundamental knowledge. Making sure you know these things is as essential as making sure that the next thriller you read does indeed contain the climactic, all-resolving, final chapter.

A pilot's tool kit can be as personal as his or her flight bag. Each of us has individual flying or working needs and preferences, not to mention little eccentricities stemming from experience or prejudices. All flight bags are likely to contain charts but not all will carry IFR charts. Some will tote manuals for simple airplanes, others for complex aircraft, depending on the pilot's level of expertise and what he can afford to fly. Similarly, the tools pilots choose as their companions tend to reflect how skillful they are and how ambitious is the work they expect to do.

There are, nevertheless, certain tools and materials that form the foundation of any efficient and flexible tool kit. They constantly are called upon for basic maintenance work and for advanced tasks. If you are just starting your career as an aircraft maintainer, you will find them well worth having. If you are an old hand at the game, read on anyway—you may well come upon some helpful new tips.

The Raw Essentials

These are the toolbox items we feel no plane owner should be without. For starters:

1. A tire gauge (dial-type preferred, but any gauge is better than none). Few tools have as short a payback period.

2. Screwdrivers for cowling and general use. A magnetic, changeable-bit driver set is ideal. (Note: Avoid cheap Phillips-head screwdrivers like those you find in the 98-cent jumble-basket at auto parts stores. Invest in a quality Phillips driver.)

3. Battery hydrometer, with numerical scale. (Stay away from the big turkey-basters and get a compact unit that'll give accurate readings using small volumes of battery fluid.) The various pilots' mail-order houses sell good, inexpensive ones.

4. WD-40 or LPS-1 penetrating oil (Mouse Milk, if you can find it). Great for freeing up ''frozen'' screws and exhaust clamps, lubricating piano hinges, etc. Stops corrosion while lubricating. (The 'WD' in WD-40 stands for ''water displacement.'' Use some on aileron hinges after a wash job; it'll drive out moisture and relubricate the hinge at the same time.)

5. Johnson's Pledge and flannel cloths for doing the windows. (You can buy Mirror Glaze or Brillianize if you want, but Pledge is

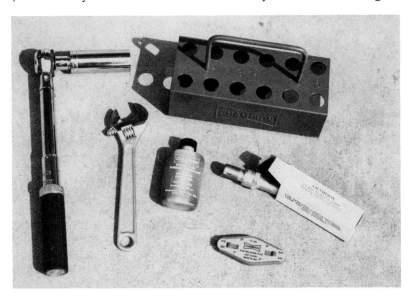

Spark plug tools are essential for getting the maxiumum life—and informa-tion—out of spark plugs. A torque wrench and 7/8-inch deep socket, plug tray, Crescent wrench, thread lube, gap gauges, and thread chaser will suf-fice for plug rotations. However, do not use the thread chaser on Helicoils (see Chapter 4).

The Sure-Gap spark plug gapper lets you set the gaps of any massive elec-trode aviation plug easily and quickly, on the ramp or in the shop. It can be carried in a shirt pocket.

safe for Plexiglas and does just as good a cleaning job, at a third the cost.)

6. Crescent wrench. (Keep at least one in the plane at all times—preferably a small one, since you'll be working in tight spaces most of the time.)

7. Pliers. (The more, the merrier. Our personal favorites are the super-small size Vise-Grips, which double for slip-joint pliers and clamps.)

8. Degreaser. (We recommend a 50:50 mix of Fantastik and water in a trigger spray bottle.)

9. Oil spout or funnel and can opener. (Keep some spare cans of oil in the plane, too.)

10. Paper towels. (Bounty brand is best for windows; otherwise, buy whatever's on special.)

Advanced Aids

So much for mere basics. On a slightly more advanced level, we would strongly suggest that all plane owners also invest in the following:

—A battery charger (12V or 24V, as appropriate). Schauer makes a dandy 24V charger, the Model K324, available through any Schauer dealer. For the 12V crowd, nearly any charger (one ampere or up) will do. It pays for itself many times over.

—A torque wrench, preferably the ratcheting (micro-adjustable) kind, reading zero to 50 foot-pounds. A 3/8-inch drive is handiest.

—A spark plug socket (for aviation use, that means a 7/8-inch deep socket, 6- or 12-point, with 2-3/8-inch working depth, minimum). Take an old aircraft plug with you when you go to the auto parts or hardware store to shop for your socket. *There is no requirement that you buy a so-called "aircraft" plug socket.*

—A long-handled wrench to loosen spark plugs. (Using your torque wrench to loosen plugs is a no-no.)

—Needle-type feeler gauges, .015 to .022-inch range.

—Plug tray.

—Spark plug anti-seize compound.

—A supply of new copper plug gaskets.

—Spark plug gapper.

—Safety wire (MS 20995 stainless, .014-inch) and wire-twisting pliers.

Owners of McCauley and Cleveland brakes can benefit from investing in relining tools. A punch and rivet set can be bought inexpensively through a number of mail-order supply firms, and spare linings are available at most FBOs. Even if you don't reline your own brakes, a ratchet/socket set can be handy.

—Oil drain hose (from your local auto parts store). Have a quick-drain installed in your sump if you don't already have one.

—Oil analysis sample bottle.

—Portable air tank (keep in your car) and/or tire foot-pump (keep in the plane). The former can be used to inflate nosegear oleo struts, if weight is put on the plane's tail.

—A grease gun (packed with MIL-G-7711 general-purpose grease), if your plane has lots of Zerk fittings. If you don't have lots of Zerks (fixed-gear Cessnas don't), skip it.

—A small jar of MIL-H-5606 hydraulic fluid (for topping off reservoirs).

—G.E. Silicone Spray (for keeping Cleveland brake anchor pins free, and for general dry-lube needs).

—Volt/ohmmeter, for electrical troubleshooting.

—Brake riveting tool, hammer, brass rivets, and spare linings (for relining brakes), if you own Cleveland or McCauley brakes. (Jacks, wrenches, and more hydraulic fluid if you own Goodyears.)

—A ratchet/socket set with 1/4-inch and 3/8-inch drives and adapters.

There are, of course, many other items that you could keep in your plane. For example, in addition to the above items, a dual mag timing light, Micromesh window refinishing kit, oil can (filled with engine oil), TR-3 Resin Glaze wax, six spare spark plugs, a jeweler's screwdriver set, a tube of RTV (silicone rubber), Microlon aerosol.

Last but not least, there's the one "tool" no plane-owner should be without: An aircraft service manual. Buy one through your local Beech, Cessna, Mooney, etc. dealer. It's money well spent.

Is it possible to have too many tools? We think not. *All tools have a payback period.* How short or how long merely depends on how many mechanics you meet along the way.

Chapter 4

GETTING TO KNOW AIRCRAFT HARDWARE

We shall now enter an area that most people whose eyes are on the skies and whose thoughts are among the clouds would rather leave to other people, those who make their living wrestling with such things as AN, MS, and NAS numbers and other technical ''gibberish.'' The nonsensical morass of cipher-like nomenclature that fills the average telephone-book-sized aircraft parts catalog literally has no meaning for the average aviator, who worries more about the Dewey Decimal System than about nut and bolt taxonomy.

That's unfortunate. A pilot who doesn't know at least something about the nuts and bolts that hold his aircraft together can never ex-

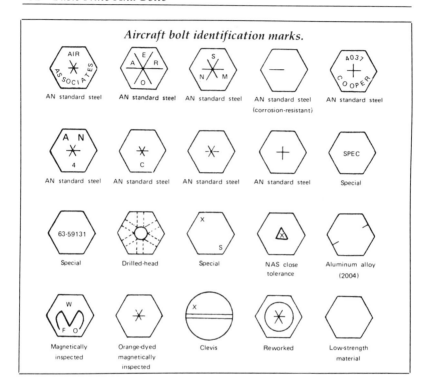

Aircraft bolt identification marks.

pect to understand such things as how to use a torque table, how to select replacement parts, when and when not to use a lock nut, and how to get the best use out of a parts catalog or service manual. For the owner who truly wants to *get into his airplane*, immersing himself in such esoterica is tantamount to paying his dues toward gaining the benefits of self-service maintenance. And it isn't all that hard to do. It merely takes willingness, concentration, and an ability to remain rooted to one's chair until the necessary learning is done.

AN, NAS, AND MS BOLTS

The vast majority of bolts used in aircraft structures are either general-purpose AN bolts, NAS close-tolerance bolts, or MS bolts. (You'll notice in your airplane's parts catalog that most bolts carry either an Air Force/Navy, National Aircraft Standard, or Military Standard specification number; that's what the abbreviations AN,

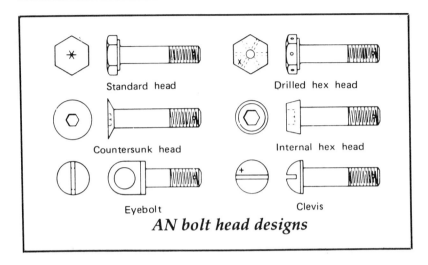

Standard head   Drilled hex head

Countersunk head   Internal hex head

Eyebolt   Clevis

AN bolt head designs

NAS, and MS refer to.) Of these three, AN bolts are the most commonly used.

AN bolts can be identified by the presence of various markings on the bolt head, as shown in the accompanying diagram. Your standard, run-of-the-parts-bin cadmium-plated-steel hex-head AN bolt will be marked with a raised asterisk or + sign, while corrosion-resistant steel AN bolts carry a single raised dash. If the bolt is made of aluminum alloy (you won't encounter many of these, since they're not used in places where they have to be removed often), there will be *two* small, raised dashes on the head. Notice that not all AN bolts are of the hex-head design; some come in clevis and eyebolt styles.

In addition to the above standard markings, the aircraft bolt's head may also carry the manufacturer's name or initials. Then too, every once in a while you'll encounter a bolt with simply a number, an ''S'', or ''SPEC'' stamped on the head. These are *special* bolts made for particular applications where ordinary AN bolts won't do the trick. If you ever have to remove one of these for any reason, *remember never to replace it with anything but the exact same item.* This goes for all aircraft fasteners (nuts, bolts, screws, etc.), of course—but it is an especially important rule to follow when working with special, or non-standard, bolts.

Very occasionally you'll come across a shiny-looking bolt with a triangle on its head; this is the NAS close-tolerance bolt. These bolts, which are made slightly oversize and then ground to a very precise diameter, are used in certain places where a *tight-drive fit* is required (that is, where the bolt will only go into the hole when struck with a 12-ounce hammer). Handle NAS close-tolerance bolts with care—replacements cost about $1.00 each (and more).

How to Decipher the Numbers

So far, we've said nothing about the numbering system that is used for classifying AN bolts. If you've ever tried to understand this numbering system and failed, you may be tempted to stop reading at this point. Don't. It's really very simple: Most of the AN bolts you'll be working with as you become more deeply involved in preventive maintenance will fall into theAN 3 through AN 20 size range, the exact AN number depending on how many sixteenths of an inch in diameter the bolt's *shank* is. If you have an AN 3 bolt, you know the shank is 3/16-inch across and fits into a 3/16-inch hole. Likewise, an AN 4 bolt is 1/4-inch in diameter, and AN 5 is 5/16-inch, and so on.

For any given shank diameter, you'll find AN bolts of various lengths, or *reaches*—which is why every AN bolt has a *dash number* (for instance, AN 5-6). This second number specifies the *length* of the bolt in *eighths of an inch*. (Notice that we're talking only about the bolt's shank length, or reach—not the overall length of the bolt). In other words, an AN 5-6 bolt would have a diameter of 5/16-inch (AN 5) and a reach of 3/4-inch (6/8-inch, dash 6). Likewise, an AN 4-7 would be 1/4-inch in diameter and 7/8-inch in length.

If you've ever had occasion to thumb through an aircraft hardware catalog (or for that matter, any airplane parts catalog), you may have noticed that there are no AN bolts with a dash number of 8 or 9. The reason: A dash number of 10 signifies a one-inch length, a ''-20'' means a two-inch reach, a ''-30'' means three inches, and so on. Which means that in all double-digit dash numbers, the last digit represents the number of eighths, while preceding digits represent the number of whole inches. In other words, an AN 7-23 bolt is 7/16-inch in diameter and 2-3/8-inch in length. Just as an AN 8-41 is a half-inch bolt with a 4-1/8-inch reach.

Now so far, all of the AN designations we have been talking about belong to bolts of the type that have *drilled tails* (for use with

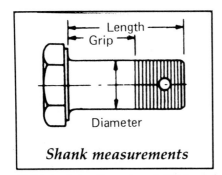

Shank measurements

castellated nuts and cotter keys or safety wire). To indicate an AN bolt with an *undrilled tail* (for use with self-locking nuts), you would simply add the capital letter 'A' to the dash number. For example, Piper Arrow main wheel halves are held together by AN 5-35A bolts (5/16-inch in diameter, 3-5/8-inch long, undrilled, for stopnut use).

Finally, there's one more type of AN designation with which you should be familiar, and that's the "H" designation. Any time you see a capital "H" between the AN number and the dash number (e.g., AN6H10A), you should know that the bolt in question has a *drilled head*. You'll see these bolts mainly in blind holes where nuts can't be used, and where—as a result—the bolt head itself must be safetied with lock wire. Some Cleveland brake installations employ head-drilled through bolts.

AN NUTS AND WASHERS

In bolt nomenclature, *both* parts of the AN number have significance; the first part (the actual "AN number" of the bolt) denotes the diameter of the bolt's shank in sixteenths of an inch, and the "dash" number expresses the bolt's grip length in whole inches and eighths. Thus, an AN 5-13 bolt would fit into a 5/16-inch hole and have a grip length of 1-3/8-inch.

The situation with AN nuts is somewhat different. In the first place, the *first* number in a nut's AN designation does not signify anything in terms of the nut's size—it merely tells you what *kind* of nut (hex, wing, castellated, not castellated, thick, thin, self-locking) you're dealing with. Thus, your AN 310 and AN 320 nuts are ordinary and shear-type castle nuts (such as you'd use with cotter pins or safety wire); AN 364 and 365 are used to designate thin and thick elastic stop nuts; AN 363 designates an all-steel stop nut (also not shown); and AN 350 signifies an aircraft-type wing nut (drilled for use with safety wire). In addition, there are the plain and light hex nuts—AN 315 and AN 340—having neither castellations nor self-locking features (you won't have occasion to deal with many of these), and their coarse-thread counterparts, the AN 335 and AN 345 nuts.

As you can see, the AN numbers of aircraft nuts bear no obvious relation to the nuts' size, composition, function, etc. If you want to know why an AN 310 nut happens to be a castle nut, you'll have to ask the Pentagon.

Happily, the *second* part of an aircraft nut's full AN designation—i.e., the ''dash'' number—does bear some relationship to reality. The main rule to remember here is that the nut's *dash*

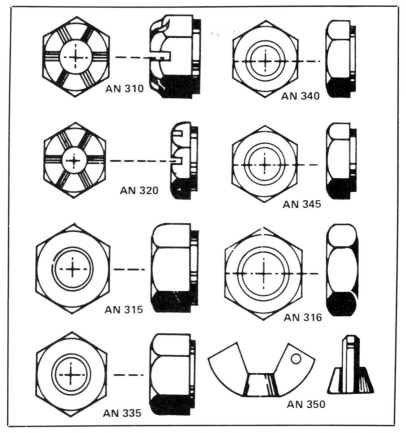

In AN nut designations, the first number indicates the type of nut that is involved. Not included here are AN363, 364, and 365 nuts.

number corresponds to the AN number (or first number) of the bolt that the nut is designed to fit. In other words, an AN 320-9 nut is designed to fit onto an AN 9 bolt, and an AN 320-8 nut is designed to fit an AN 8 bolt, and so on. The nut's dash number does *not* represent the exact diameter of the threaded hole portion of the nut—the nut is several thousandths larger than the bolt (it has to be, or the nut wouldn't turn down onto the bolt to begin with). So don't try to tell a mechanic that an AN 320-4 nut has a 1/4-inch-diameter hole in it, or you'll find yourself the object of some merry-making.

Frequently, the second number of a nut's AN designation is three or four digits long (you'll see this quite often in your plane's parts catalog). Here, the last two digits of the dash number specify the *number of turns of thread per inch* (or thread pitch), while the one or two preceding digits call out the nut size (the bolt size, really) in sixteenths of an inch. For instance: You may find (by looking in your parts catalog) that the wheel halves of each main wheel on your plane are held together using AN 365-524 nuts. You would automatically know, from what we've just said, that a nut of this kind would go on an AN 5 bolt, 5/16-inch in shank diameter, and has a thread pitch of 24 turns per inch.

Thread pitch is often called out in the dash number for the simple reason that two main types of threads—fine (American National Fine series) and coarse (American National Coarse)—are in common use. (Then too, there are American Standard Unified Coarse and American Standard Unified Fine series nuts in use, also.) This is important, because you have to know the thread pitch of a nut before you can look up its recommended torque value (about which, more shortly).

Nut Designs

We have mentioned that drilled-shank bolts are made to be used with castle nuts (but not with elastic stop nuts), while undrilled bolts—the ones that carry a suffix "A"—are used with stop nuts, but not with castle nuts. Nothing was said, however, about just *why* these various nut/bolt combinations are used where they are. One might wonder, for instance, why stop nuts aren't used *everywhere* (making safety wire unnecessary on nuts and bolts), inasmuch as the FAA already allows them to be used in many critical applications (such as to hold wheel halves together).

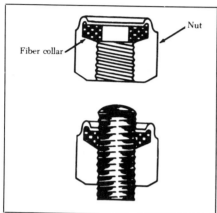

An AN365 stop nut with a nylon ("fiber") insert that resists the loosening effects of vibration.

To understand why castle nuts and cotter pins (or safety wire) are used in some places and lock nuts in others, it's necessary, first, that you understand something of the *design* of nuts. (Form, after all, follows function.) Let's begin with elastic stop nuts.

Basically, your ordinary, run-of-the-goodie-bag AN 365 stop nut is nothing more than a standard hex nut that's been increased in height to accommodate a *nylon insert*. This insert—which is un-threaded, and securely embedded in the top of the nut—can be exposed to oil, gasoline, carbon tetrachloride, ether, and other solvents without ill effect (which means you needn't rush out and buy a replacement if you happen to drop one of these jewels into a pail of Super Clean-All). The insert is also very stiff, although it won't hurt bolt threads or plating.

Incidentally, these nylon inserts come in a variety of colors. The Air Force says the different hues signify different heat-resistance qualities. For civilian purposes, though, never mind the color.

The nylon (or "fiber") insert is there to help keep the load-carrying edges of the nut and bolt threads in positive contact at all times and at all torque values. You'll see how this works when you try to thread a stop nut onto a bolt. At first, you'll be able to spin the nut on with your fingers—but when the tip of the bolt reaches the tough nylon collar, you'll be forced to turn the nut the rest of the way down with a wrench. And as you do so, the steel threads of the bolt will cut into the nylon insert, creating extra friction and *forcing the insert upward, thereby placing a load on the bolt's threads*. Once in place, no amount of vibration will cause the stop nut to unscrew itself spontaneously.

Where are elastic lock nuts commonly used, then? Anyplace where there's vibration—which is to say, all over the aircraft.

"But doesn't nylon become soft at high temperatures?" you may be thinking. Yes indeed. Fiber-insert nuts of the type we've just been talking about lose their "self-locking" quality at around 250°F. (You won't find any of these nuts in your plane's exhaust system.) To cope with this limitation, the people who make aircraft hardware offer something called an *all-steel* "high temperature" lock nut (AN 363), which comes in cad-plated and stainless steel versions. These beauties have a threaded *metal* insert that performs the same function as the nylon-type insert (although in a slightly different manner). And they perform well at high temperatures.

Vibration can't loosen a self-locking nut, but it stands to reason that an *applied torque* might. Hence, it doesn't make sense to use a stop nut (regardless of the type of insert) for any application in which either the nut or the bolt is subjected to rotational forces. It makes better sense, in such cases, to use a nut/bolt combination that can be *safetied* with lock wire (MS20995) or cotter pin (MS24665, AN 380, AN 381). Hence the castle nut (AN 310, 320).

Look at your plane and you'll find that castle nuts are used to secure drilled bolts wherever two parts that turn with respect to one another meet. Landing gear torque links, axles, clevises, and control linkages are examples of areas requiring castle nuts and drilled bolts secured with safety wire (or cotter pins).

Believe it or not, there's even such a thing as a *self-locking castle nut* (MS17825), which is just what it sounds like; a castle nut manufactured to standard specifications, with a nylon insert for added safety. (Even if—Wichita forbid—the cotter pin *breaks*, this baby will *still* stay put!) Because these nuts cost a good bit more than ordinary castle nuts and stop nuts, you won't come across them very frequently; they're generally found only in areas that demand the ultimate in fail-safe operation (such as the control system).

Before we leave the topic of nuts, let's be sure to get one thing straight: Castle nuts can be used and re-used indefinitely (barring damage to the threads, of course), but *elastic stop nuts do wear out*. Stop nuts *can* be removed and put back on many times, but there eventually comes a time when the nylon insert is so well "broken in" that it no longer provides sufficient thread compression to lock the nut. The FAA says that when this point is reached—that is, when you find you can spin the stop nut all the way onto the bolt with just your fingers—the nut must be dispatched to the nut graveyard. (Find out where the most frequently disassembled stop nuts are on your aircraft—the wheel halves, for example—and order some replacements now, so you won't be caught short when replacement time comes. It can come very suddenly.)

The Washer Requirement

Finally, a word about washers: *Some* kind of washer (usually an AN 960 or AN 970 flat washer) will be found beneath almost every nut and bolt head you examine. (The FAA *requires* washers to be used on all nuts and bolt heads unless their omission is specified by manufacturers' service publications.) Usually, however—because aircraft nuts are either self-locking or are secured externally—*lock washers* are not used, and, in fact, their use on aircraft primary and secondary structures is forbidden. So if you find a bolt or nut on your airplane that has no washers on it at all—or that has lock washers instead of flat washers (or *more than one flat washer* under any one nut or bolt head)—be suspicious. Consult a mechanic.

Also, of course, consult an A&P if you discover any elongated bolt holes (this is not uncommon on wheel and brake assemblies), bolts with worn shanks, failed safety wire or missing cotter pins—in general, anything that has a questionable appearance.

NUT/BOLT TORQUE

The FAA is not content to let mechanics (or pilots, or anyone else) tighten aircraft nuts and bolts until they're damn well *tight*, as is common practice in auto garages. Instead, the FAA makes it clear—in several of its publications for mechanics—that every nut-bolt combination must be *torqued* to its ideal tightness.

Proper torquing of nuts and bolts is more important than you probably realize. *Under*-tightening of nuts/bolts can cause unnecessary chattering, leading to premature failure of the bolt and/or elongation or destruction of bolt holes and bushings. (You see this all the time with wheel halves and brake torque plates.) *Over*torquing can cause permanent damage to nuts, bolts, and/or underlying aircraft structures—more easily than you might imagine. (Given enough leverage, a child of six can strip a half-inch bolt.)

But there's more going on here than simple under-tightening or over-tightening. As the speed of an aircraft increases, the stresses placed on that aircraft's bolted-together structures increase dramatically (often in exponential fashion). Thus, what may have started out as a small difference in load-bearing ability (i.e., bolt tightness) on the ground can quickly turn into a *large* difference in actual stresses experienced by structural members when the aircraft is flying at 150 knots (and maybe pulling a couple of extra g's, too). In such a situation, some portions of the affected structure are going to absorb more stress than others—perhaps more stress than the design will allow.

The only way that you can know for sure that the loads placed on your plane's bolted structures are being distributed evenly—the only way you can be fairly certain that the nuts and bolts that are holding you up won't suddenly quit doing their job—is to see to it that all the nuts and bolts you come in contact with are properly torqued.

Always remember one thing: Every nut and bolt you take apart will have a *minimum and a maximum recommended torque value* for reassembly. Frequently, the appropriate torque values will be stamped on the part or structure from which the nut and bolt came; this is often true of wheel halves, for instance. Failing that, the torque range will usually be given in the appropriate manufacturer's service manual, or in service bulletins. (Avco Lycoming publishes torque limits for its engines and accessories as a special service publication: *Service Table of Limits and Torque Tightening Limits,* SSP2070-3, available from Lycoming distributors. Teledyne Continental discloses its torque limits in its various overhaul manuals, as well as in TCM Service Bulletin M75-3.)

How to Use the Standard Torque Table

If you can't find specific torquing recommendations (or a generally applicable torque table) in the appropriate manufacturer's service publications, you can still arrive at the proper torque value(s) for your nut and bolt by means of the FAA's Standard Torque Table. To use this table, you need merely know the AN number of the bolt you're working with (which you can get very quickly by measuring the bolt's shank diameter and converting it to sixteenths of an inch), the AN or MS number of the nut, and the bolt's thread pitch in turns per inch (eyeball it). You also need to know if the nut and bolt are made of steel or aluminum; 90 percent of the time it will be steel. Of

STANDARD TORQUE TABLE (FAA)

BOLTS

Steel Tension	Steel Tension	Aluminum
AN 3 thru AN 20	MS 20004 thru MS 20024	AN 3DD thru AN 20DD
AN 42 thru AN 49	NAS 144 thru NAS 158	AN 173DD thru AN 186DD
AN 73 thru AN 81	NAS 333 thru NAS 340	AN 509DD
AN 173 thru AN 186	NAS 583 thru NAS 340	AN 509DD
MS 20033 thru MS 20046	NAS 624 thru NAS 644	MS 27039D
MS 20073	NAS 1303 thru NAS 1320	MS 27039D
MS 20074	NAS 172	
AN 509 NK9	NAS 174	
MS 24694	NAS 517	
AN 525 N K525		
MS 27039	**Steel shear bolt**	
	NAS 464	

NUTS

Steel Tension	Steel Shear	Steel Tension	Steel Shear	Aluminum Tension	Aluminum Shear
AN 310	AN 320	AN 310	AN 320	AN 365D	AN 320D
AN 315	AN 364	AN 315	AN 364	AN 310D	AN 364D
AN 363	NAS 1022	AN 363	NAS 1022	NAS 1021D	NAS 1022D
AN 365	MS 17826	AN 365	MS 17826		
NAS 1021	MS 20364	MS 17825	MS 20364		
MS 17825		MS 20365			
MS 21045		MS 21045			
MS 20365		NAS 1021			
MS 20500		NAS 679			
NAS 679		NAS 1291			

STANDARD TORQUE TABLE (FAA) FINE THREAD SERIES

Nut-bolt size	Torque Limits in-lbs. Min.	Max.	Torque Limits in-lbs. Min.	Max.	Torque Limits in-lbs. Min.	Max.	Torque Limits in-lbs. Min.	Max.	Torque Limits in-lbs. Min.	Max.	Torque Limits in-lbs. Min.	Max.
8–36	12	15	7	9	--	--	--	--	5	10	3	6
10–32	20	25	12	15	25	30	15	20	10	15	5	10
1/4–28	50	70	30	40	80	100	50	60	30	45	15	30
5/16–24	100	140	60	85	120	145	70	90	40	65	25	40
3/8–24	160	190	95	110	200	250	120	150	75	110	45	70
7/16–20	450	500	270	300	520	630	300	400	180	280	110	170
1/2–20	480	690	290	410	770	950	450	550	280	410	160	260
9/16–18	800	1,000	480	600	1,100	1,300	650	800	380	580	230	360
5/8–18	1,100	1,300	660	780	1,250	1,550	750	950	550	670	270	420
3/4–16	2,300	2,500	1,300	1,500	2,650	3,200	1,600	1,900	950	1,250	560	880
7/8–14	2,500	3,000	1,500	1,800	3,550	4,350	2,100	2,600	1,250	1,900	750	1,200
1–14	3,700	4,500	2,200	3,300	4,500	5,500	2,700	3,300	1,600	2,400	950	1,500
1-1/8–12	5,000	7,000	3,000	4,200	6,000	7,300	3,600	4,400	2,100	3,200	1,250	2,000
1-1/4–12	9,000	11,000	5,400	6,600	11,000	13,400	6,600	8,000	3,900	5,600	2,300	3,650

COARSE THREAD SERIES

Nut-bolt size	Torque Limits in-lbs. Min.	Max.	Torque Limits in-lbs. Min.	Max.	Torque Limits in-lbs. Min.	Max.	Torque Limits in-lbs. Min.	Max.	Torque Limits in-lbs. Min.	Max.	Torque Limits in-lbs. Min.	Max.
8–32	12	15	7	9	--	--	--	--	--	--	--	--
10–24	20	25	12	15	--	--	--	--	--	--	--	--
1/4–20	40	50	25	30	--	--	--	--	--	--	--	--
5/16–18	80	90	48	55	--	--	--	--	--	--	--	--
3/8–16	160	185	95	110	--	--	--	--	--	--	--	--
7/16–14	235	255	140	155	--	--	--	--	--	--	--	--
1/2–13	400	480	240	290	--	--	--	--	--	--	--	--
9/16–12	500	700	300	420	--	--	--	--	--	--	--	--
5/8–11	700	900	420	540	--	--	--	--	--	--	--	--
3/4–10	1,150	1,600	700	950	--	--	--	--	--	--	--	--
7/8–9	2,200	3,000	1,300	1,800	--	--	--	--	--	--	--	--
1–8	3,700	5,000	2,200	3,000	--	--	--	--	--	--	--	--
1-1/8–8	5,500	6,500	3,300	4,000	--	--	--	--	--	--	--	--
1-1/4–8	6,500	8,000	4,000	5,000	--	--	--	--	--	--	--	--

course, if you have a parts catalog for your plane (which you should), all of this information will be at your fingertips.

Let's say you're putting your nose wheel back together and you need to know how tight to torque the through bolts, but the bolt torque is not given on the wheel halves and you've forgotten to bring your plane's part catalog with you. How do you determine the bolt's torque range? First, you find the diameter of the bolt's shank. If (as is likely) you find that it is 1/4-inch across, you'll know automatically that the bolt is of the AN 4 variety. (A 5/16-inch bolt is an AN 5, etc.) Next, determine whether the nut is a thin lock nut (AN 364), an ordinary lock nut (AN 365), or a castle nut of some kind (AN 310 or AN 320). You'll probably find that it's an ordinary lock nut: AN 365. You determine by visual inspection that both the bolt and nut are made of steel.

Now get out your ruler once more and count the number of threads on the bolt's tip for every inch of reach. A pitch of 28 threads per inch would put this particular nut/bolt combo in the "fine thread" series. Which means that all you have to do now is find the column of the Standard Torque Table that contains AN 4 (actually, AN 3 through AN 20) bolts, run your finger down the page to the "nuts" column containing your AN 365 nut (that's the left-hand column), then keep moving your finger straight down the page until—in the part of the table labeled "Fine Thread Series"—you encounter the nut-bolt size of 1/4-28. Directly across from 1/4-28, you'll find the numbers 50 and 70. Those numbers represent the minimum and maximum torque limits (in inch-pounds) for your nose wheel through bolts. (Note: To convert to foot-pounds, simply divide inch-pounds by 12, giving you—in this example—4.17 and 5.83 foot-pounds.)

Notice that the torques given in the accompanying table are for *unlubricated nuts and bolts. The use of grease, solvents such as gasoline or kerosene or Stoddard solvent (all of which leave a film residue when they dry), or anti-seize compounds, or such common freeing agents as WD-40, Liquid Wrench, etc., will lead to improper torquing of the nut and bolt,* thus rendering the assembly unairworthy. If you know or suspect that your nut or bolt's threads are coated with any kind of solvent, by all means wash the affected parts in methyl chloroform or methyl ethyl ketone or acetone (which do not leave a film when they dry) before torquing everything.

Naturally, whenever you torque *any* bolt, you should try to tighten the *nut* down onto the *bolt*, rather than place your torque wrench on the bolt head. If, however, you're screwing a bolt into a blind hole—or for some reason you can't reach the nut, and you *must* turn the bolt head—always torque the bolt to the higher torque limit. (When you rotate the whole bolt, the wrench is working not only against bolt torque, but against the friction of rotation as well. This causes the desired torque to be reached prematurely. To correct for this, it's necessary to use the higher torque value.)

In all other cases, of course, you should tighten the nut to a torque value midway between the two limits—*unless* you find it necessary to go higher or lower in order to line up nut castellations with drill holes.

SAFETYING TECHNIQUES

In the course of performing your own maintenance, you can expect that you will have to reassemble a nut, bolt, clevis, or other piece of hardware and then *safety* it, either with safety wire or a cotter pin. According to the FAA, all non-self-locking fasteners used in aircraft primary structures *must be externally secured*, to ensure that they will not suddenly depart the aircraft (at least not without some difficulty). If you intend to install an oil filter, for instance, you will have to safety it. In fact, knowing how to safety both safely and expeditiously is an essential part of preventive maintenance.

Although safetying is a basic operation, even professional mechanics can be guilty of sloppy, and therefore potentially damaging, work. For example, when we recently examined the work of a major East Coast shop, we were surprised to see a CH48109 oil filter safety-wired not to the adapter base (where spin-ons are supposed to be wired), but to the engine's rear-mounted *oil cooler*. The wire run—from the hex of the Champion filter can to the crossbrace on the back side of the cooler—was over a foot long; and the wire was pulling sideways on the (long-reach) filter.

In this section, we will discuss proper safetying in general and also focus on applying the techniques to oil filter installation. We will also offer tips on safetying with cotter pins.

Probably, the most common type of safetied fastener you'll have occasion to deal with is the ordinary castle nut (AN 310 or 320), which is used in conjunction with drilled bolts. Safetying one of these gems is easy—providing you can get the nut's castellations to line up exactly with the hole in the tip of the bolt after tightening the nut down to its proper torque. This can be more of a problem than it would first seem, since [1] castle nuts are not ''keyed'' (i.e., the hex doesn't clock to the threads). and [2] close adherence to recommended torque values will often prevent slots from lining up properly.

There are ways, naturally, of dealing with this situation. The first thing you can do is try torquing the nut to its minimum recommended torque value, then tighten the nut slowly in an attempt to get things to line up before reaching the *maximum* allowable torque. If the moon and tides are with you, proper alignment will occur before you reach the higher torque value.

The second thing you can do (providing the above procedure does not work) is to try a *different washer* under the nut. Frequently, the substitution of a new washer for an old, flattened one will do the trick. If not, you can substitute a new washer of a different *thickness*. (AN 960 flat washers come in two different thicknesses, to deal with just this situation. The thinner washers can be identified by the presence of a suffix 'L' on their dash number: an AN 960-7L is a thin-series 7/16-inch flat washer.)

Of course, one thing you definitely will *not* want to do is use two (or more) washers where there was only one to begin with. The FAA allows no more than one washer per nut (or per bolt-head).

Should the foregoing techniques fail to produce the desired alignment between castellation and bolt-hole, you have one more option—and that's to try an entirely new castle nut, OR an entirely new bolt (or both). Remember, a castle nut's threads are not keyed, and the AN 310 nut that didn't work on this bolt will work on another somewhere else.

After you've achieved alignment between the castellations of the nut and the hole in the bolt, you can begin to secure the assembly with safety wire or a cotter pin—whichever was there to begin with. If you need to use wire, choose the largest diameter wire that will fit through the bolt hole (you can get safety wire in several sizes). You will need to use aircraft-quality stainless steel wire with ''MS20995'' printed on the spool. Do not use the barnyard-grade stuff you see so often at hardware stores.

It is important to consider the metallurgy of the hold-down point versus the wire itself. Simply put, you don't anchor a stainless-steel wire run to an aluminum or brass oil cooler. Not only can vibration cause the harder metal to chew into the softer one, but galvanic interaction may occur (leading to corrosion damage). Fortunately, when dissimilar metals do crop up, you don't *have* to resign yourself to using stainless wire on non-steel parts. Aircraft-grade MS20995 safety-wire is available not only in Type 304 (soft temper) stainless, but in annealed brass (QQ-W-321) and other metals as well, in sizes ranging from .032-inch and .041-inch (the most commonly used diameters) to .048 and .060—or as tiny as .020-inch if you like.

Again, for a given job, use as large a size of wire as will pass through the work. Strength is definitely a consideration, so the bigger the better. Always use *new* safety wire for each job.

The Right Tool

What sort of tool is best for safety-wiring? No one seriously questions the superiority of lockable, pull-to-twist, semi-automatic cutting/twisting pliers (the $75 type that professional mechanics use), as exemplified by the Milbar 1W. Any number of manufacturers offer these pliers—in various lengths, jaw angles, etc.—with and without automatic return. Bigger isn't necessarily better where safety-wiring tools are concerned, however, since you'll often be working in tight areas. A 10-inch Milbar 1W (with automatic return) is just right.

Duckbill pliers—the original safety-wiring tool—will also work, if you're an artist with wire and you've got all day. Then again, for light-duty work there's always the ACS-made screw-driver-type wire twister (at $7.95 or so), which takes less skill than duckbills but requires some getting-used-to. Our advice is to splurge on a Milbar 1W (or equivalent). The savings in time and aggravation on blind wire runs will quickly make up for the super-twister's high acquisition cost (and don't forget, it doubles as a pair of dikes).

Safetying Imperatives

FAR Part 43, Appendix A specifically allows pilots to replace defective safety-wire, more or less without restriction, but we'd urge you to leave turnbuckles and control-system items to your

Essentials for safetying: MS 20995 stainless safety-wire and a Milbar 1W twister/cutter.

A&P. Everywhere else, simply bear in mind the cardinal rules of safety-wiring:

1. Keep runs taut, with 6 to 12 twists per inch. (One twist equals 180 degrees of wrist action.)

2. Always configure the wire so it pulls on the bolt head (or whatever) in a *tightening* direction.

3. Never put more than three bolt heads, clevises, studs, etc. on a single twisted run.

When can you simply thread a single (untwisted) piece of wire through adjacent bolts or clevises?

The FAA allows single-wiring of small screws, closely spaced bolts, parts in electrical sysems, and any parts that are extremely difficult to reach. The maximum number of parts in a single-wire series is limited to the number that can be connected by a 24-inch piece of wire. (This is spelled out in AC 65-9A.) Again, it's important to run the wire in a *tightening* direction: i.e., pulling any piece of wire directly away from the work should result in the wire wanting to cinch up (clockwise-rotate) the work. (Naturally, if you're dealing with anti-clockwise threads, you'll want to run the wire in the appropriate direction.)

The Procedure

If you've never wired anything before with a pair of professional twisters, here's the procedure:

First, identify the point(s) you'll be connecting with wire, and guesstimate the length of wire needed. Remember that a double-stranded run requires a piece of wire equal to twice the work length, plus about 15 or 20 percent for take-up (the wire "shrinks" as it's twisted), *plus* an adequate margin for a pigtail and gripping with the pliers.

Second, with the oil filter (or to-be-wired item) out of the way, loop the untwisted wire through the ultimate anchor point (i.e., the base pad, if you're doing an oil filter). Bring exactly half the wire through the anchor. Try to minimize bending or flexing of the wire.

Next, install the oil filter or bolt(s), etc., to be wired, and torque as required. Do not over- or under-torque to make wire holes line up.

Now look and see how much distance there is from the anchor point to the tie-point on the work itself. Pull the wire with your fingers until your fingertips are opposite the intended tie point; keep going another 15 percent or so (for take-up); then, at exactly this location, grab both strands of wire with your twisting pliers. Lock the pliers by squeezing them and sliding the locking collar into place.

The idea now is to twist the length of wire—exercising the pull-to-twist feature of the special pliers—to give the desired 6 to 12 turns per inch, with all turns ending *just short* of the intended (distal) tie point on the work. In other words, when you've finished twisting the run, you should end up with a 'Y' whose nexus barely reaches the tie point. What you want to be able to do is thread *one* arm of the 'Y' through the work, continue the other arm *around* the bolt-head (if that's what you've got), mate up the two arms again, and twist them together. (Relocate your pliers as necessary to accomplish this.)

It's important to continue twisting well past the final anchor or loop point. Generally, a pigtail of half an inch is sufficient. (Be

Safety-wiring can begin at either of this Cleveland caliper's through-bolts.

Lock the pliers on at a point adjacent to the distal bolt.

Pull to twist (6 to 12 turns per inch).

careful cutting off the excess wire—flying wire shrapnel is extremely hazardous to unprotected skin and eyes.) Bend the pigtail around the hex, if a hex is present, or back and out of the way if no hex is present. Avoid grazing your arm against the sharp pigtail.

Things to remember: [1] Your twists should be tight and even but not *too* tight. Beginners have a tendency to over-twist the wire, resulting in a very taut run between anchor points. You don't want to work-harden the safety wire to the point where normal airframe vibrations will cause it to fail. [2] Be sure to bend your pigtails back or under so that there's no danger of them snagging other parts, or scraping your skin. (Sharp-pointed pigtails can cut like razor blades.) [3] Don't pick anchor points at random. [4] Don't make long runs when short ones will do. [5] Don't accept sloppy work. Start over if you have to. Safety-wire is cheap. Sloppy work never is.

Speaking of sloppy work, the flawed oil filter installation mentioned earlier provides some helpful pointers about such safetying work.

Given that short wire runs are generally preferable (all else being equal) to long wire runs, AC-brand spin-on filters could be considered preferable to Champions, since AC types come with wire loops at the base band, whereas the only wiring provisions on a Champion are at the tack-welded hex at the top of the can. (In other respects, the two filter types are essentially equivalent.)

A good safety-wire run takes the shortest possible path to the nearest acceptable anchor point. In the above example, there were 13 or 14 inches of run where six or eight would have sufficed (had the pad wiring point been utilized). Instead of wiring the filter to the pad (a vertical run), the horizontal orientation of the wire imposed a sideward stress on the filter at the location of maximum moment-arm. But there's another reason to favor wiring to the pad rather than a nearby object: The pad vibrates with the filter, whereas other points on the engine vibrate in other directions (not necessarily in phase). Engines shake when they run (especially on start-up and shutdown) and unless

Pass one strand through the work and lock on again.

When cutting the pigtail, be careful to guard against flying fragments.

The finished run should be taut, in the direction of tightening.

Champion spin-ons tend to require long runs. Wiring to the oil pan is accep-table here.

the anchor point for the wire shakes with the accessory, you've got the potential for breakage.

Cotter Pins

Thankfully, the installation of cotter pins offers less opportunity for foulups than safety-wiring. Even so, you'll want to watch what you're doing. Cotter pins come in a variety of lengths, diameters, and alloy types; and as you know, they also come in aircraft and non-aircraft types. You want only brand new, never-been-used-before MS24665 or AN 380 aircraft quality cotter pins.

Some rules-of-thumb to remember when working with cotter pins:

[1] Check to be sure the pin fits neatly into the bolt hole *with little or no side-play.*

[2] Start the prongs apart with a screwdriver, then tap them lightly with a mallet to get them to bend. Do not make any sharp bends.

[3] See that the top prong (the one bent back over the end of the bolt) does not extend beyond the bolt diameter . . . by cutting the prong back, if necessary.

[4] See that the lowermost prong does not rest against the surface of the washer, or the assembly adjacent. (Again, trim the prong back.)

[5] If you wish, you can bend the prongs around the sides of the nut, instead of bending one up and one down. In this case, be certain the ends of the prongs do not extend outward from the nut hex.

Once you get the hang of it—with some experience under your belt—you will probably come to regard safetying as a snap and not an adventure. Just keep your wits about you and your standards of performance high.

HANDLING MAJOR THREAD REPAIRS

Replacing bolts or nuts that have thread damage is seldom budget-threatening. But damaged internal threads on such parts as cylinder heads and crankcases are significantly more frightening. Terrifying, some would say.

Typically, the need for repair to internal threads is the direct result of a hamfisted amateur (or even a hamfisted professional) cross-threading a bolt or screw or—heaven forbid—a spark plug. Or, just as commonly, a loose stud erodes away the original threads. After

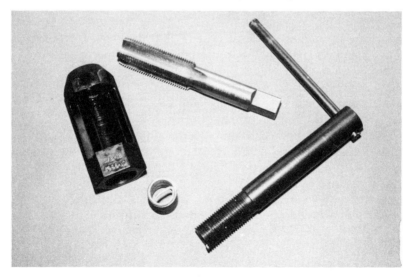

Basic Helicoil-installing tools include tap, mandrel, threaded coil driver, and sample coil (notice the tang).

citing the appropriate ex-
pletives and running a tap
through the threads to clean
them up, one often finds that
the problem won't fix itself.
The cost of cylinder heads
and crankcases being what
they are, it is hardly practical
to throw away thread-
damaged components. For-
tunately, there are several
repair alternatives recognized
by the FAA.

This photo shows the relationship of the Helicoil to the driving tool body.

The first repair op-
tion—particularly for an exhaust stud—is to install an oversized
replacement stud. (This calls for dressing the hole with the proper-
size tap, choosing from among half a dozen or more commonly
available stud oversizes, and installing the stud.) The second option
is to install a bushing, which must be staked into place and then
threaded to accept a stud. The third option—and the most common
repair by far—is to grab a Helicoil kit and install an insert.

The Helicoil, invented in the late 1930s by Harold Caminez, is a
precision-formed screw thread coil of 18-8 stainless steel wire that
has a diamond-shaped cross-section. The coils—called inserts by the
manufacturer, the Helicoil Division of Emhart Fastening Systems
Group (Shelter Rock Lane, Danbury, CT 06810)—each has a driving
tang that is notched to facilitate tang removal after installation is
complete. (The complete process is described below.)

Helicoils are used in the manufacture of missiles, aircraft engines
and accessories, and in many applications that employ tapped
threads in light metals (particularly where there is a need for frequent disassembly). They come in National Coarse or National Fine
threads, and in metric and pipethread sizes, in a bewildering
number of diameters and depths. For repair purposes, they're even
referenced in the FAA's *Airframe and Powerplant Mechanic's General
Handbook*, AC 65-9A.

Installation Procedure

Installing a Helicoil is simple enough: By far the most difficult aspects of the operation are [1] gaining access to the damaged part, and [2] maintaining perpendicular alignment when tapping new threads.

Here's the general procedure, which is further explained by the accompanying photographs:

1. After disassembly as needed to gain access to the damaged hole (and after determining the dimensions of the threads), drill out the threads to the minimum depth specified in the Helicoil kit; the bolt threads must engage the entire length of the Helicoil to assure maximum strength. The generally accepted standard for material dimensions is that the wall or casting (base; substrate) should have a thickness one and a half times the diamcter of the Helicoil, although in reality Helicoils are available for use with material depths of just one Helicoil diameter. In the case of the insert depicted in the accompanying photos, it was necessary to drill a 41/64th-inch hole. If at all possible, chuck the part in a lathe or use a drill press. Barring that, rig a guide of some sort. Otherwise, if you're using a hand drill-motor, proceed with caution and be careful not to elongate the hole or drill it at an angle. Repairing a hole that already has an existing (and damaged) Helicoil is by far the simplest type of repair: Merely remove the old insert, using a double-edge extraction tool, which you tap with a hammer to seat it, then unscrew counterclockwise.

2. After the hole is bored, is must be tapped with the tap supplied with the kit. If you want to have a real mess on your hands, run the tap in at an angle. Blow out or otherwise clear away metal chips from the hole. Tip: When drilling or tapping aluminum castings, use a lubricant consisting of one part lard oil, or other animal oil, to two parts kerosene. This will prevent overheating of the metal and tearing of threads.

3. Retract the mandrel from the tool body and place the insert into the well. Note that the tang must be located so that the mandrel will be threaded all the way through the insert to engage the tang with the tooth on the mandrel. Go ahead and rotate the mandrel through the insert until the tang is fully engaged. Then continue turning the mandrel until the insert is within a thread or so of beginning to come out the tool body.

4. Place the tool squarely against the tapped hole and hold it with one hand while turning the mandrel until the threads engage in the new threads you have cut in the part. Continue turning until the top

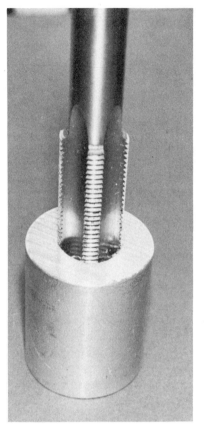

This photo sequence shows how to install a spark-plug Helicoil (a sample plug of metal is used here for demonstration purposes): First, using the tap to thread the hole into which the Helicoil will go; second, installing the coil in the hole; third, the properly installed Helicoil.

of the insert is a quarter to a half thread below the top surface. It's important to realize that you must allow the installation tool to *float*, without holding it tightly against the work surface. Nowhere is it suggested that any sort of thread-lock compound is necessary, but Loctite is inexpensive, and a drop or so surely can't hurt. It is not

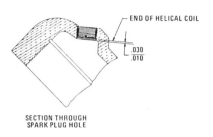

SECTION THROUGH
SPARK PLUG HOLE

Spark plug coils should stop approximately .030-inch short of the bottom of the hole.

necessary to use special corrosion-protective measures with aluminum castings in normal environments (Continental installs stainless-steel Helicoils in aluminum cylinder heads all the time); but with magnesium, it's imperative. For corrosion protection in both aluminum and magnesium, the most common material available in the field is zinc chromate primer. Coat the insert with zinc chromate and run it into the threaded hole while still wet. And be happy, for zinc chromate is recommended for extremely severe corrosion environments.

5. After the Helicoil is installed, back the mandrel out of the hole, and break off the installation tang. The manufacturer recommends using a punch or rod of a diameter that just fits into the assembled insert. Needle-nose pliers can also be used to bend the notched tang until it breaks off. The punch must have a square end with a chamfer; it is inserted until it rests on the tang, then it is struck sharply with a hammer. Retrieve the tang to avoid a bolt or stud bottoming against it in the hole before it is tight.

Afterwards

If you are making a spark-plug-hole installation, it is absolutely essential that the end of the Helicoil not protrude into the combustion chamber (where it will create a hot spot that could cause preignition). Continental calls for spark-plug inserts to "bottom out" .010 to .030-inch *before* reaching the bottom of the tapped hole.

Of course, if you're installing a new Helicoil in a spark plug hole, it's probably because the old one backed out with the spark plug when you were doing your last plug change. What causes backing

Helicoil and Special Tool Data
(Teledyne Continental Motors)

Thread Size	Basic T.C.M. Part No.	Helical Coil Corp. Part No.	Drilled Hole Diameter	Helical Coil Special Tap No.* Rough	Fin.	Helical Coil Thread Plug Gauge No.	Helical Installing Standard	Coil Tools Prewind	Tang Break-Off Tool	Heli-Coil Extractor
1/4-20	24323-4	1185-4	.261-.266	186-4	187-4	188-4	724-4N	528-4N	1195-4	1227-6
5/16-18	24323-5	1185-5	.328-.333	186-5	187-5	188-5	724-5N	528-5N	1195-5	1227-6
3/8-16	24323-6	1185-6	.390-.395	186-6	187-6	188-6	724-6N	528-6N	1195-6	1227-6
7/16-14	24323-7	1185-7	.453-.458	186-7	187-7	188-7	724-7N	528-7N	1195-7	1227-16
18mm	520112	C2-52	.718-.723	2-22		2-1	—	543	—	1227-16

Notes: *For aluminum alloy castings. For numbers of taps designed for steel refer to the manufacturer's bulletin No. 650-R.

T.C.M. Part Numbers: To basic part number add "B" for phosphor bronze, or "C" for stainless steel. Add -1, -1.5, or -2 for length equal to nominal diameter times 1, 1-1/2, respectively. (All T.C.M. furnished inserts are notched.)

Heli-Coil Part Numbers: To basic part number, as listed, add "B" for phosphor bronze, or "C" for stainless steel and "N" for a notched insert, if desired. Add "X" and length desired, expressed as a fraction of an inch. Example: 1185-5CN x 15/32 represents a 5/16-18 N.C. insert of stainless steel whose length is 15/32 inch, or 1-1/2 times its nominal diameter.

out? Generally one of two things: Overtorquing the plug on the previous installation, or failure to maintain clean threads (i.e., carbon crust buildup on spark plug threads caused the plug to "freeze solid" to the Helicoil). The appropriate preventive measures are obvious. Use a torque wrench when installing plugs (go no further than 30 ft-lbs), and *be sure all threads are clean* before screwing plugs down. Also, lube the threads sparingly with engine oil or graphited thread lube.

Installing a Helicoil doesn't take long. The hardest thing about making the sample installation shown here was finding a 41/64ths drill bit. Installing a Helicoil insert actually takes less time than reading about it.

Because of the large variety of sizes of inserts, it is probably impractical to buy a tool for each repair. Better to borrow than to stock up on mandrels. The inserts themselves are only pennies each—unlike the parts that they permit you to salvage.

Part III
INSPECTIONS

Chapter 5

ACCEPTANCE AND PRE-PURCHASE CHECKS

In the course of your life with your airplane, there will be many inspections, most of which you will perform yourself. They make the airplane truly yours. But they are not limited to preflight walkarounds and postflight checks of problems detected in the air. To keep your ship healthy, periodic investigations leading to preventive maintenance will be made. Looming above them all will be the inevitable annuals, which could cost you a bundle each time, unless your own examinations and fixes eliminate work the inspecting mechanic doesn't have to do.

Before you begin this relationship, however, an introductory inspection is called for—a cold, hard, penetrating look inside and out before you put your brand on your new airplane, be it a mint-new or used.

THE ACCEPTANCE EXAMINATION

Let's say, first, that your steed is hot off the assembly line, spanking new and gleaming with but a few hours' ferry-flight time from the plant. It beckons you to sign the papers, rush on board and, on wings of faith, assume full ownership and head for the sky. Our experience-founded advice: Stop, take a deep breath, and start probing, for immediately upon taking legal possession you will be alone not only with the delights of your airplane but with problems that may lie hidden beneath its glossy exterior.

The Defect Epidemic

Date: August 15, 1979. Aircraft: Cessna T210M. "Oil temperature thermocouple bulb was found connected to cylinder head temperature gauge. Cylinder head temperature thermocouple connected to oil temperature gauge." Total time on aircraft: 187 hours.

Date: August 29, 1979. Aircraft: Cessna 172N. "On [initial] inspection of the aircraft, lower engine mount to engine bolt was found missing.'' Total time: 17 hours.

Date: June 12, 1979. Aircraft: Cessna 182Q. ''Left rudder cable was wrapped around right rudder cable twice, and once around elevator cable between stations 32 and 74.'' Total time: 100 hours.

There is a tendency among new-plane buyers to assume that a ''ferry time only'' aircraft, because it *is* new, should be squawk-free. Or, if not entirely without flaws, at least *airworthy*. Certainly (the new-plane buyer's thinking goes), there can be nothing *major* wrong with a brand-new airplane; after all, the plane's construction is monitored every step of the way by quality-control inspectors (one out of twelve Piper employees, for example, is an inspector), it is test-flown by factory pilots *after* construction, and in all likelihood the new plane is given an additional ''once over lightly'' inspection by the dealer or distributor on acceptance. What could possibly be wrong with a new plane, except perhaps for a little paint overspray here and there, or the usual avionics ''crib death'' problems?

The answer: Plenty.

In reviewing a full year's worth of FAA Service Difficulty Reports, we are particularly disturbed by [1] the sheer *number* of manufacturing and assembly irregularities reported to the FAA, [2] the very serious nature of many of the incidents cited, and [3] the fact that a good many safety-of-flight defects are not discovered until the plane's first, second, or even its third 100-hour or annual inspection.

In terms of numbers, we're talking in the neighborhood of eight to twelve FAA Service Difficulty Reports a month involving manufacturing/assembly errors in new aircraft (versus a total issuance of 65 to 100 SDRs per month). It now appears that *approximately 10 percent of all service irregularities reported to the FAA's Maintenance Analysis Center in Oklahoma City center around assembly defects in new aircraft.* As if this isn't bad enough, various sources estimate that less than 10 percent of all significant service irregularities discovered in the field are reported to the FAA on Form 8330-2 (Malfunction or Defect Report) . . . which means that for every incident that makes it to the stage of an FAA Service Difficulty Report, nine or ten (or perhaps 20 or 30) similar occurrences were probably observed, but not reported to the FA7. Thus it is likely that *80 to 120 manufacturing and assembly errors affecting safety are turning up in the field every month in the U.S.* (Wichita's *total output*, by comparison, is only 1,500 units a month.)

For what it's worth, the vast majority of ''assembly defect'' reports received by *Light Plane Maintenance* every month involve Cessna aircraft (of various models) and Piper Tomahawks. Assembly-defect reports are rarely received for Mooney and Beech products . . . perhaps because Mooney and Beech service personnel do not report such problems to the FAA. (Malfunction and defect reporting is done on a voluntary basis only.)

What Can Be Wrong

Some of the assembly defects that have been reported recently have been quite egregious. In addition to control cable misrouting (which appears to be quite common, as assembly errors go, among high-wing Cessnas), we have instances in which essential parts are simply omitted during construction, parts are installed improperly (fasteners crossthreaded, circuit breakers installed with insufficient panel clearance to allow breaker opening, etc.), and—on occasion—instances in which parts are ''force-fitted'' into position. The FAA recently cited an instance in which a Cessna 185 with 9 hours TTSN was found to have a kinked metal fuel line (kinked, apparently, at the factory):

''The fuel input line to the fuel strainer was found bent and kinked. It was reported that the bend probably occurred during installation as a result of the line not being formed to fit the installation during fabrication. The kink reduced the cross-sectional area of the line by approximately 50 percent. *The replacement part had to be reformed for proper installation.''* (FAA AC 43-16, September 1979)

Recently, at least two Cessna aircraft (one 207 and one 185F) suffered melting of the pitot-static tubing inside the cockpit *where the plastic tubing had been routed against cabin heat ducting.* One aircraft was flying in instrument flight conditions when the ''meltdown'' occurred. Both planes were low-time.

Two cases were recently reported in which fuel hoses on low-time aircraft were found chafing against engine exhaust components. In one case, chafing had proceeded to the point where raw fuel was being sprayed on exhaust stacks. (The owner of the plane had complained to his mechanic of a persistent gasoline odor in the cockpit. Were it not for this, the man might have gone on flying.)

More than one instance of hydraulic-line misrouting and chafing has been reported for new retractable-gear aircraft. To cite just one

A bright and shiny new airplane creates an impression of flawless design and construction. The harsh truth remains that a squeaky-clean machine is still a collection of vulnerable parts assembled and examined by fallible humans.

occurrence, a Cessna 210N with 82 hours TT was reported as having a severely chafed gear-up hydraulic line (P/N 128050991). The actual Service Difficulty Report states:

"Gear up hydraulic line was found chafed in center console support. On gear-up cycle hydraulic fluid leaked over center console components."

We could continue to cite assembly-defect horror stories (based on actual Service Difficulty Reports) *ad infinitum*—or at least *ad nauseam*. The point is that [1] brand new aircraft are *not* always free of defects (far from it), and [2] the types of defects that can be—and *are being*—found in new aircraft are frequently quite serious, serious enough to warrant an exceedingly thorough "acceptance inspection" *on delivery of the aircraft to the buyer*, before the plane is actually placed in service.

The Inspection Agenda

We suggest that anyone who takes delivery of a new aircraft (or demonstrator aircraft) conduct an exhaustive inspection covering *at least* the following items: 1. Aircraft controls (for proper operation, cable routing, and security of all components), including all engine and propeller controls.

2. Powerplant, exhaust system, and ignition system (for proper installation, clearance, and operation). Spark plug wires should not chafe against exhaust components or cylinder fins, nor should they contain sharp bends. (The ignition leads on new Cessnas are sometimes drawn up much too tight.) Exhaust risers should not be kinked, cracked, or show evidence of hammering into place. Connections should be secure.

3. Flexible fluid lines (for proper routing, security, and general condition). Check all fuel and oil lines for proper fit and absence of chafing. Thoroughly inspect all hydraulic lines to landing gear for security and clearance from control cables. 4. Pitot-static plumbing (for proper routing, security, and general condition). Ensure that tubing is routed well away from cabin heat ducting.

5. Electrical equipment and avionics (for proper installation and operation). Ensure that bare terminals—at the alternator, battery, solenoids, etc.—are not in contact with other materials. Check cir-

The temptation for a new owner to sign the papers, do a quick walk-around and then taxi out for that blissful first flight can be overwhelming and deadly. Check everything that can be checked before you accept and fly.

An acceptance check resulting in this wing condition would be somewhat extreme, but do peer into hidden inspection areas for alien objects.

cuit breakers for adequate panel clearance. Check ignition switch and magneto P-leads for proper operation (by ground-running the engine, turning the switch to OFF, and seeing that the engine does, in fact, quit running). Ensure that antennas are properly connected to black boxes.

6. Landing gear, wheels, tires, brakes, and associated equipment (for proper installation and operation). Retractable-gear aircraft: Jack airplane and perform retraction-cycle check. Check clearances of gear doors, arms, springs, struts, and forks during all phases of the up and down cycles. Fixed-gear aircraft: Check gear attach points for security. (On July 31, 1979, a Cessna T188C ag-plane with 32 hours total time experienced *left main gear separation* on landing rollout. Saddle bolt P/N MS20008-58 ''and related parts'' were missing.)

7. Exterior and interior surfaces and equipment, including seats, baggage containment structure, doors, windows, emergency exits, ELTs and cockpit lights (for proper installation, security, and

operation). Check to see that shipping screws have been removed from ELT activation switches. Cabin-class twins: Check emergency window installations. (It has been found that on some Cessna 400-series and Piper PA31-series aircraft, emergency exits cannot be opened due to interference created by card tables and/or other cabin furnishings.)

8. Tail cone, fairings, cowlings, and hidden inspection areas (for loose rags, screwdrivers, hardware, and/or other materials overlooked on final close-up).

You'll notice that since the foregoing inspection is *not* of a type required by law, and since none of the above items call for disassembly of any primary operating system (inspection, yes; disassembly, no), a mechanic is *not* needed to perform an acceptance check. The inspection may legally be performed by the pilot/owner himself (or herself). This is, in the purest sense of the word, preventive maintenance.

If you have just taken delivery of a new aircraft—or plan on doing so soon—we urge you to perform a thorough acceptance check (in accordance with the above guidelines) *before* placing the aircraft in service. *Do not* wait until your first scheduled 100-hour inspection—or even your first 25-hour inspection—to see whether your wings are bolted on tight. They might not be. (And don't take anyone else's word for the plane's mechanical integrity. The fact that the dealer *says* the plane was inspected before it was sold doesn't mean anything.)

Incidentally, if you want to read the pertinent FAA Service Difficulty Reports for yourself and prove to your own satisfaction that major assembly defects do indeed occur in general aviation aircraft, write to the FAA, AAC-23B, AFS-581, P.O. Box 25082, Oklahoma City, OK 73125. (For a search and setup fee—the FAA's Safety Data people will give you a computer printout of any kind of service difficulty information you want. Write and state your needs.)

YOUR OWN PRE-PURCHASE INSPECTION

There are lots of cheap used aircraft on the market now, but many of these aircraft—perhaps most of them—could hardly be called a "bargain" in terms of after-sale maintenance. Many owners sell because they can't afford to keep their airplanes airworthy and in license. It's not unusual for a plane to come onto the used market after months or years of neglect, during which time hundreds or *thousands* of dollars' worth of maintenance squawks may have piled up. These squawks, naturally, will someday have to be taken care of by the plane's new owner—and that could be you, unless you learn, *before* you buy, how to evaluate a used plane's true maintenance status.

BIG EXPENSE ITEMS:	
	Exhaust system
	Engine mount
Turbocharger	Simmonds fuel
Turbo controller	injectors
Propeller	Gear saddles
Engine (internal)	Goodyear brakes
Airframe corrosion	Dope & fabric work
Autopilot	Wood repairs
Deicer boots	(airframe)
Fuel cells	Paint job
	Upholstery

SMALL EXPENSE ITEMS:	
	Prop governor
	Strobes, lights
	Flight instruments
ELT	Shimmy dampener
Tires	Oleo strut seals
Batteries	Microphone
Cleveland brakes	Cabin loudspeaker
Master cylinders	Cockpit headliner

Detective Work

Everyone knows that the first thing you do when you're checking out an airplane for prospective purchase is study the logbooks. Scrutinize the airframe and engine (and propeller and accessory) logs, and find out what the total engine time is . . . what the airframe time is . . . who did the last major overhaul . . . what the TBO status of the propeller, fuel injector, turbocharger, and/or other accessories is . . . when the next annual is due . . . and which airworthiness directives have been complied with.

Then start finding out the true facts. To do this, you'll need to engage in a little detective work. Call or visit the mechanic who has been doing most of the plane's regular maintenance; ask him what *he* thinks of the aircraft . . . and of the previous owner. What kind of customer was the owner? Did he insist on first-class maintenance? Have all factory bulletins been complied with? (Have *any* factory bulletins been complied with? Which ones, specifically?) Just as important: has the plane seen frequent use, or has it been grounded throughout much of the year?

If possible, talk with the people who did the last engine overhaul. If the overhaul came prematurely (for example: the airframe total time is 1,300 hours, but the engine is 575 SMOH), attempt to find out why. Were any warranty claims ever submitted on the engine? Was anything unusual found at teardown? Which parts were replaced? Was the overhaul done to new tolerances, or service limits?

If the engine is super-low-time (less than 200 SMOH), ask about oil consumption. (Check it yourself on a test flight, if you can.) An engine that's still burning a quart every couple hours at 200 SMOH very likely hasn't broken in properly—and never will. You may be looking at glazed cylinders and an expensive hone job.

If the engine has been through several previous majors, find out how old the core is. (Look at the logs, not the tach.) Are the crankshaft, crankcase, and/or cylinders more than two majors or 3,000 hours old? If so, you may well be looking at an extraordinarily expensive overhaul when TBO rolls around again. (After all, you can't keep regrinding crankshafts and rechroming cylinders forever.)

Visual Clues

If your initial research fails to turn up anything earthshatteringly interesting, give the airplane a thorough visual once-over. Sight down rows of rivets, looking for the occasional zigzag or odd pattern that could indicate field repairs performed after a hard (or gear-up) landing. Examine faying surfaces for bulges indicating trapped corrosion. Look for the halo of dirt that announces a loose rivet. And wherever there's fuel, look for stains indicating chronic leakage.

In the engine compartment, look for oil leaks—but don't expect to actually find any until after your first demonstration flight. (The seller may have just washed the engine.) Look for white, gray, or brown stains on exhaust components (signs of leakage). Look for fuel stains on or around induction-system components. Oil dripping from the induction drain tube may signal worn intake valve guides. (Anything dripping from anything generally spells trouble.)

Oil analysis reports, if available, will give you some idea of the engine's internal health—although it should be mentioned that a less-than-forthright seller can provide the buyer with a misleading picture of engine health simply by obtaining analyses from several different labs and hiding the worst reports. The thing to do, if you're able, is to draw a small sample of oil from the filler neck or dipstick tube of the engine in question, and send it off for analysis to the lab of your choice. If you get a phone call from the lab a few days later saying your oil is full of silicon (dirt) and copper (from bearings), you'll be glad you invested in spectrum analysis, even if it was only on a one-time "shot in the dark" basis.

Unusual Problems

In addition to the more or less standard maintenance checkpoints just listed, you'll want to scrutinize your prospective purchase for all the special mechanical glitches that are endemic to that particular plane type. The way to get a handle on this is to contact the FAA's Flight Standards National Field Office in Oklahoma City for a Service Difficulty Report printout on

You can pay a mechanic a hefty sum to inspect your prospective purchase for you, but if you know what to look for, it is better to take off the cowling and do the initial examination yourself. Then, if you still want to buy the airplane, arrange for an annual inspection at the time of sale.

the type of plane (or engine) you're interested in. The FAA will send you a printout of SDRs by type or model of plane, by engine, or by accessory, going back a maximum of five years. In fact, if you want, they'll even search the records by "N" number, allowing you to see if the plane you intend to buy has itself ever been written up for an unusual defect. Write to: FAA/DOT, AFO-580, P.O. Box 25082, Oklahoma City, OK 73125.

Mechanical Coverups

You'd probably be amazed at the number of mechanical discrepancies that can be artfully "covered up" by a crafty used-plane salesperson. Oil leaks, as mentioned before, can be obscured by washing the engine down before showing it. Exhaust stains around cowl openings (a sure indication of leaky connections and/or blown gaskets) can simply be removed with commercial degreaser. Ditto for belly oil (under-fuselage grime, indicating an oil-burning engine).

Large mag drops can be done away with by "bumping" the timing up a few degrees—a fairly common (although dangerous) practice. Oleo struts that repeatedly go flat can be aired up—or over-aired—just before a sale. Likewise, leaky brake master cylinders can be tidied up and serviced with hydraulic fluid at the last minute.

An engine with low oil pressure (indicative of pump and/or bearing wear) can be made to have higher oil pressure instantly by means of a simple adjustment to the oil pressure relief valve. (On some engines, you can "dial in" more oil pressure merely by turning a setscrew; on others you have to replace a spring or add washers.) The grade of oil makes a difference here, too. The thicker the oil, the higher the indicated oil pressure.

Even aircraft performance can be faked. Normally, one of the best indications of a sick or worn-out engine is lack of takeoff, climb, and cruise performance at gross weight. If a plane has a constant-speed prop, however, poor engine (and aircraft) performance can be compensated for by simply tweaking the prop governor to give 50 or 75

A used plane that has been used mainly on the ramp is potentially a lemon. If the aircraft hasn't been exercised in flight at least 180 hours over the past 12 months, decrepitude may have set in.

more rpm. Some airspeed indicators read higher than others, too, and it doesn't cost much to put a high-reading gauge in a slow-cruising plane.

None of this is to suggest that used-plane dealers are, as a group, in any way underhanded or dishonest. Most are not. The point is simply this: There _are ways_ of covering up a doggy plane's weaknesses—and in today's economic environment, there are substantial incentives for used-plane sellers (be they professional or amateur) to take advantage of every available trick in "unloading" a hard-to-sell plane. It doesn't hurt anyone—except maybe a dishonest seller—for you to know what some of these tricks are.

Acid Test

Is there no acid test, or tests, by which one can reliably evaluate the mechanical condition of a used plane's engine (or other systems)? As it turns out, there are, indeed, some mechanical-soundness indicators that can't be faked or fooled with. To get a handle on these, you have to fly the airplane.

Start by checking the oil. Note precisely the amount of oil in the sump at the start of the flight; then arrange to recheck the oil afterwards with the airplane sitting on the same spot, with the same amount of nose strut extension. (This will have a marked effect on dipstick readings for many planes.)

Next, fly the plane for at least one hour, preferably at high cruise-power settings. (If the aircraft is turbocharged, go to critical altitude to check turbo system performance. Failure to achieve certificated critical altitude is a tipoff to possible problems with exhaust or induction leaks, automatic controller components, and/or the wastegate or turbocharger itself.) During your flight, note at least the following things:

1. Rigging: With hands and feet off the controls, does the airplane want to fly straight?

2. Flight instruments: do they all work? This is not a big-expense area (see box), but worth paying attention to nonetheless.

3. Noise and vibration: Unusual noises/vibrations are sometimes tipoffs to imminent engine, mount, prop, exhaust, or other problems.

4. Radios: Turn them all on and check them. Try the VORs on several frequencies and in both TO and FROM directions in all

quadrants. (Crosscheck one against the other, and both against a ground reference, to determine accuracy.) Talk to ATC and verify the transponder code readout. Ask for a Mode C (altitude) readout, too.

5. Autopilot: Does it work? Put its capabilities to the test. This is a potential major expense, should repairs be needed.

6. Engine instruments: Are all indications in the green? Does oil pressure fall off after an hour at high cruise? (It will sag somewhat, normally, but not into the low-low green.)

7. Turbo system: Can you reach critical altitude? Is roughness apparent above 12,000 feet (indicating ignition problems)? Do you encounter bootstrapping (unstable manifold pressure) at high altitudes?

Upon landing, taxi straight to the ramp and shut down (before the plugs have had a chance to "load up"), noting the rpm rise as you slowly retard the mixture control. A rise of more than 50 rpm means the idle mixture is set too rich. No rise—or a rise only with carb heat—means the mixture is set too *lean*. Continued sporadic running after mixture cutoff signals an internally leaking carburetor or fuel injector.

At this point, if you're really serious about wanting to know engine health, step outside and remove all the engine's top spark plugs. The firing ends should be dry. Oil wetness on top-hole plugs generally means oil has been escaping past piston rings (due possibly to advanced ring or cylinder-wall wear). An engine in need of a top overhaul generally will have wet plugs, top and bottom.

Don't forget to give the engine compartment a thorough postflight inspection, to detect oil leaks—and other glitches—that may have escaped your attention before. And don't forget to pull the dipstick. Oil consumption on your test flight should have been negligible.

Myths for Gullible Buyers

To maintain a sound purchasing perspective, it should help to consider nine myths about used planes that many buyers tend to believe. These are selling points that can bring a lemon into your life:

Myth No. 1: Low total time is desirable in a used plane. To the contrary: idleness is a plane's worst enemy—especially forward of the firewall. Lycoming says, for example, that its engines will go to full

TBO only if they're flown at least 15 hours per month. By this criterion, a 1976 aircraft with less than 1,000 hours TTAE (or any plane that's flown less than 180 hours in the preceding 12 months) is suspect; you may be looking at a premature overhaul. If the choice is between a plane that's been flown regularly and one that hasn't, take the former every time.

Myth No. 2: High total time is unacceptable. This may be true in special cases, where life-limited components are involved. As a general rule, however, high time does not automatically mean mechanical or structural unsoundness. What counts is not total time, but condition. If an engine (or whatever) can be shown to be in good condition—correct tolerances, normal wear rates, etc.—who cares how much time it has?

Myth No. 3: Logbooks never lie. Logbooks give, at best, a very incomplete picture of an engine's or airframe's service history . . . not only because logs do, in fact, sometimes lie, but because—more often—they simply fail to tell the truth, the whole truth, and nothing but the complete truth. Unlogged work is exceedingly common. It's the rare mechanic, after all, who religiously enters every oleo strut air-up in a plane's logs; and yet, *without* such log entries, how is a prospective buyer to know that the plane in question might have a history of oleo stuts repeatedly going flat? This is the problem facing the used-plane buyer. Generally speaking, if you find you can't determine (by reading the logs) who last serviced the oleo struts—or installed the tail strobe light, say—you can assume that other, perhaps more important, work has been done to the plane without being logged.

Myth No. 4: "No damage history" means no damage history. As mentioned above, unlogged work—repair work, even—is common. Technically, of course, this isn't supposed to happen. Major repairs require the filing of FAA Form 337 with both the FAA and the aircraft owner. Likewise, minor repairs are supposed to be entered in the plane's logs, in accordance with FAR 91.173. However, FAR 91.173-(a)(1) provides that such records need not be retained after one year. Thus, if a plane incurred damages resulting in minor repairs, the records for those repairs (if more than a year old) could legally have been disposed of some time ago, in which case you could (jokingly) say that the plane now has no damage *history*. Further complicating this issue is the FAA's precise definition of "major alterations,'' which leaves out such things as total replacement of an aileron. The important thing to remember is that *damage* is not required to be recorded in a plane's logs at all; only the subsequent repairs are. So if you read ''propeller replaced this date'' in a logbook, you have no way of knowing *why* the prop was replaced. Did the owner merely want to upgrade propellers? Or did the previous prop suffer a close encounter with a Chevrolet?

Myth No. 5: ''All ADs complied'' means all ADs complied. Read logbooks carefully for wording. Some mechanics log airworthiness directives in a manner that fails to meet the exact requirements of FAR 91.173(a)(2)(v) . . . despite the fact that if these requirements are not met, the AD, in effect, has not been properly complied with. Also, ADs are often poorly worded and thus open to misinterpretation. Thus, many ADs that should be complied with aren't, simply because some A&P has decided the aircraft ''isn't affected by serial number.'' The best way to check AD histories is to look up the ADs

Any pre-purchase annual should be performed by the purchaser's mechanic, not the seller's, and the seller should be willing to bear some fraction of the costs—ideally 50 percent. If the seller wants to forego the annual in lieu of promises on paper, consider what those promises actually will be worth when the inspection finally is made.

yourself (at your local FBO; or you can buy the whole mess from FAA AAC-23, P.O. Box 25461, Oklahoma City, OK 73125) . . . and read logbook entries yourself, carefully. *Don't* take anyone else's word for it—and for sure, don't accept a written guarantee. The fact that someone's willing to give you a written guarantee of AD compliance doesn't necessarily mean the ADs have been complied with. It means, rather, that the seller is anxious to close the deal.

Myth No. 6: "Recent annual" is a worthwhile selling point. Ballpoint maintenance knows no bounds at the time of a sale; therefore, be extremely wary of any "recent annual," particularly if little documentation (parts tags, receipts, etc.) can be found. Also remember that a recent annual is not always the same as a *good* annual. How do you know that all discrepancies were, in fact, fixed at the last annual? You don't, obviously. So what you want is not a *recent* annual, but an annual at the time of sale—done by your mechanic, not the seller's.

Myth No. 7: "Low time since major overhaul" is a truly desirable thing. Who majored the engine? What parts were replaced? (How old is the existing crankshaft? Crankcase?) Was the engine overhauled to new tolerances, or service limits? These questions are ultimately more important than how many hours the engine has since major. Again, what counss here is *the condition of the engine*—not some number written in a logbook.

Myth No. 8: A Part 135 aircraft is more desirable than a Part 91 aircraft. You often see the claim "aircraft presently operated Part 135" in ads, as if the maintenance afforded an air-taxi aircraft were somehow better than the maintenance given planes operating under Part 91. This simply isn't true. (Read your FARs.) In fact, in some cases the reverse is true; it depends on the operator. About the only thing you can be sure of with a Part 135 aircraft is that it's been through the wars.

Myth No. 9: New paint is always good. Not so! A cheap paint job nearly always subtracts from the value of the aircraft, even if it doesn't blister and peel within six months—which it often will.

No Guarantees

You can ask for a written guarantee of the plane's soundness at the time of sale, if you want. Frankly, we wouldn't bother. Once the sale has been made, the ball is in your court. If discrepancies are found later and your used-plane broker is 500 miles away, all you'll have to show for your efforts is a piece of paper with someone's guarantee on it—and a broken airplane.

Your best guarantee of avoiding a lemon is to check the prospective purchase out yourself—and get expensive squawks fixed *before* you sign the papers. In used-plane sales—as in used-car, used-home, and used-anything-else sales—the byword is *caveat emptor*. Which, translated from the Latin, means roughly: *Do a complete maintenance audit before you buy.*

Chapter 6

ANNUAL INSPECTIONS

Like death and taxes, annual inspections appear to be with us for the duration. There's no escaping them. The FAA, it is true, has recently relaxed the periodic inspection requirements for homebuilt aircraft (so that it is now possible for the owner-builder, under certain conditions, to perform all required inspections himself, without consulting an AI-rated A&P or an FAA maintenance inspector), but the prospects for a parallel relaxation of the periodic inspection rules relating to normal-category aircraft appear to be nil at the moment.

Thus, annual inspections will continue to be the single largest disruptive force in the average plane-owner's maintenance budget, second in financial impact only to unscheduled engine maintenance.

This is not to say, however, that annual-inspection costs cannot be controlled, manipulated, moderated; there are, in fact, many ways (some well-known, others not) of holding the line on annual-inspection costs. One of the best ways to keep costs down is to do some shopping around before deciding on a particular maintenance facility to do the annual—and by this we do not mean merely calling various shops for essentially meaningless ''estimates'' (based on flat rates), then choosing the cheapest one. Shopping for an annual is quite a bit more complicated than this.

THE NATURE OF THE ANNUAL

One complication can lie in an owner's not knowing exactly what constitutes an annual inspection in the eyes of the FAA. Is a cylinder compression check mandatory? Must the oil be drained from the engine? Is it required that radios and autopilots be checked? The answers to these and other questions are contained in Appendix D of FAR Part 43. If you have never read Appendix D, we urge you to do so now, for it will greatly aid your understanding of what an annual inspection is and is not. It will not only make shopping for good service at lower cost more rational, but it will also be a useful guide if you perform your own pre-annual inspection. Here is Appendix D in its majestic entirety:

Scope and Detail of Items (as Applicable to the Particular Aircraft) to be included in Annual and 100-Hour Inspections.

(a) Each person performing an annual or 100-hour inspection shall, before that inspection, remove or open all necessary inspection plates, access doors, fairing, and cowling. He shall thoroughly clean the aircraft and aircraft engine.

(b) Each person performing an annual or 100-hour inspection shall inspect (where applicable) the following components of the fuselage and hull group:

(1) Fabric and skin—for deterioration, distortion, other evidence of failure, and defective or insecure attachment of fittings.

(2) Systems and components—for improper installation, apparent defects and unsatisfactory operation.

(3) Envelope, gas bags, ballast tanks, and related parts—for poor condition.

(c) Each person performing an annual or 100-hour inspection shall inspect (where applicable) the following components of the cabin and cockpit group:

(1) Generally—for uncleanliness and loose equipment that might foul the controls.

(2) Seats and safety belts—for poor condition and apparent defects.

(3) Windows and windshields—for deterioration and breakage.

(4) Instruments—for poor condition, mounting, marking, and (where practicable) for improper operation.

(5) Flight and engine controls—for improper installation and improper operation.

(6) Batteries—for improper installation and improper charge.

(7) All systems—for improper installation, poor general condition, apparent and obvious defects, and insecurity of attachment.

(d) Each person performing an annual or 100-hour inspection shall inspect (where applicable) components of the engine and nacelle group as follows:

(1) Engine section—for visual evidence of excessive oil, fuel, or hydraulic leaks, and sources of such leaks.

(2) Studs and nuts—for improper torquing and obvious defects.

(3) Internal engine—for cylinder compression and for metal particles or foreign matter on screens and sump drain plugs. If there is weak cylinder compression, for improper internal condition and improper internal tolerances.

(4) Engine mount—for cracks, looseness of mounting, and looseness of engine to mount.

(5) Flexible vibration dampeners—for poor condition and deterioration.

(6) Engine controls—for defects, improper travel, and improper safetying.

(7) Lines, hoses, and clamps—for leaks, improper condition, and looseness.

(8) Exhaust stacks—for cracks, defects, and improper attachment.

(9) Accessories—for apparent defects in security of mounting.

(10) All systems—for improper installation, poor general condition, defects, and insecure attachment.

(11) Cowling—for cracks, and defects.

(e) Each person performing an annual or 100-hour inspection shall inspect (where applicable) the following components of the landing gear group:

(1) All units—for poor condition and insecurity of attachment.

(2) Shock absorbing devices—for improper oleo fluid level.

(3) Linkage, trusses, and members—for undue or excessive wear, fatigue, and distortion.

(4) Retracting and locking mechanism—for improper operation.

(5) Hydraulic lines—for leakage.

(6) Electrical system—for chafing and improper operation of swiches.

(7) Wheels—for cracks, defects, and condition of bearings.

(8) Tires—for wear and cuts.

(9) Brakes—for improper adjustment.

(10) Floats and skis—for insecure attachment and obvious or apparent defects.

(f) Each person performing an annual or 100-hour inspection shall inspect (where applicable) all components of the wing and center section assembly for poor general condition, fabric or skin deterioration, distortion, evidence of failure, and insecurity of attachment.

(g) Each person performing an annual or 100-hour inspection shall inspect (where applicable) all components and systems that make up the complete empennage assembly for poor general condition, fabric or skin deterioration, distortion, evidence of failure, insecure attachment, improper component installation, and improper component operation.

(h) Each person performing an annual or 100-hour inspection shall inspect (where applicable) the following components of the propeller group:

(1) Propeller assembly—for cracks, nicks, binds, and oil leakage.

(2) Bolts—for improper torquing and lack of safetying.

(3) Anti-icing devices—for improper operations and obvious defects.

(4) Control mechanisms—for improper operation, insecure mounting, and restricted travel.

(i) Each person performing an annual or 100-hour inspection shall inspect (where applicable) the following components of the radio group:

(1) Radio and electronic equipment—for improper installation and insecure mounting.

(2) Wiring and conduits—for improper installation and poor condition.

(4) Antenna including trailing antenna—for poor condition, insecure mounting, and improper operation.

(j) Each person performing an annual or 100-hour inspection shall inspect (where applicable) each installed miscellaneous item that is not otherwise covered by this listing for improper installation and improper operation.

The Big Picture

Annual inspection costs are complicated and are influenced by a number of factors, some of which can militate heavily against the cost-cutting techniques mentioned below. There are some factors that—when added (or multiplied) together—virtually *guarantee* an expensive annual despite the owner's best attempts to reduce costs. It is important for you to know what these factors are, so that you

All airplanes are not created equal; neither are they inspected that way. This twin is bound to cost more to annual than the single-engine fellow Cessna with which it shares the hangar.

can eliminate those that are under your control—and come to grips with those that aren't.

Take a moment to answer the following questions:

1. Have you owned your present airplane less than one year? Will the next annual be the first one that you have bought for this plane?

2. Is the plane a light twin?

3. Will you have the plane annualed by a different shop this year? (Or will you be taking the plane back to the same shop that did last year's inspection?)

4. Do you live in or near a large metropolitan area?

5. Has the aircraft received frequent care throughout the year? Are all squawks up to date?

6. Will any AD notes come due for the first time with the next inspection?

7. Has the engine/engines accumulated more than 500 hours since the last top or major overhaul?

8. Is the airframe more than 20 years old?

Obviously, there are no "right" or "wrong" answers to these

questions. However, it can be said that (with the exception of question 5) the more "yes" answers you gave to the foregoing questions, the more expensive your next annual inspection is likely to be.

Let's examine the questions one by one:

1. If you've owned your present aircraft less than a year and have never "lived through" an annual inspection with it, your first inspection may cost you quite a bit more than you expected. (This is assuming you bought the plane used, not new.) The reason is that used airplanes are very often allowed to deteriorate for months before they are put on the market. The purchaser, of course, usually discovers the most glaring squawks before, during, or immediately after the sale, but other, less-easy-to-detect problems almost always come to light at the next annual inspection. (Don't let the fact that the plane was sold on the basis of having had a "recent annual"—or a "fresh annual"—fool you into thinking the plane is clean. Unless you personally attended and supervised the previous annual, you have no way of knowing what kind of surprise will crop up at the next inspection.)

2. Obviously, if you own a complex aircraft—such as a twin—you can expect to have more expensive annual inspections than you would if you owned a plane of lesser performance. Many first-time twin owners are surprised at just how expensive annual inspections can be for this class of airplane, despite the owner's best attempts to save money. There are ways to cut costs with twins as with singles, but the point is, there is no sense kidding oneself into believing that a twin-engine annual can be had for single-engine prices, It can't.

3. Switching from one maintenance facility to another is a good way to drive up annual-inspection costs, since each shop does things a little differently from the next, and a shop seeing a particular airplane for the first time is more likely to give it an exhaustive going-over than if the plane has been in and out of the same shop numerous times before. (In addition to checking truly important items, a strange shop may well examine your cabin carpeting, the cockpit speakers, door moldings, etc. before returning the plane to service.) This is not to say that there aren't good reasons, in many cases, to switch maintenance facilities from one year to the next. It *is* to say that once you find a shop you trust and like, it pays to stick with it from year to year (until you have a good reason to go elsewhere).

4. Maintenance facilities at large airports (and at small airports near large cities) do tend to be more expensive, on the average, than shops located in sparsely settled areas. Also, looking at the country as a whole, shop rates tend to be lowest in the southeast and highest in the southwest and northeast. (Alaska and Hawaii are not included in this discussion.) The best shop rates can be found in the sparsely settled parts of Georgia, Tennessee, Alabama, Mississippi, and the Carolinas. Don't rule out the possibility of flying several hundred miles in order to get a better rate on your next annual inspection. (Many Florida plane-owners travel to North Carolina each year to have required inspections done because labor rates are so low there.)

5. The key to keeping annual-inspection costs down, of course, is to keep squawks to a minimum—and the only way to do this is *fix all squawks as they come up during the year*. (Here, we're talking not just about squawks directly affecting airworthiness, but also such things as worn tires, worn spark plugs, low oleo struts, batteries, etc.) There is no more expensive way to fix a squawk than to wait till the end of the year and have it fixed at annual-inspection time. FBO shops love nothing more than to charge Joe the Bonanza Owner $20 apiece (and $25 an hour) to install new spark plugs in his plane during an annual inspection—spark plugs that Joe could have bought elsewhere at 40 percent off and installed himself for nothing before wheeling the bird into the shop (assuming he in fact needed new plugs, which he may not have; many perfectly good plugs get thrown out at annual time). When it is possible to do so, it pays to give your plane a *pre*-annual inspection, to catch any last-minute squawks that might be more inexpensively fixed *before* the plane gets sent to the shop.

6. You may have noticed that many airworthiness directives are written in such a way that compliance is not required until the plane's next periodic inspection comes due; this has the effect of causing unpleasant surprises at annual-inspection time. Also AD notes have a way of remaining dormant for several years before suddenly and unexpectedly popping up during an inspection. (It sometimes takes mechanics several years to figure out that a certain magneto AD or prop AD was never properly complied with.) The way to avoid surprises here is to research your plane's ADs yourself—something you should be doing on an ongoing basis

already. You can order a complete backfile of AD notes (for all planes under 12,500 pounds) from the FAA—and get a two-year subscription to new AD notes. (Request the *Summary of Airworthiness Directives for Small Aircraft, Volume 1,* Stock No. 050-007-00425-7 from the Dept. of Transportation/FAA, P.O. Box 25461, ACC-23, Oklahoma City, OK 73125.) It pays (literally) to read airworthiness directives carefully and see that they are complied with properly. Often, an AD note will target magnetos or other items made only during a certain time period (for instance, "Airborne dry vacuum pumps made between March 15, 1979 and June 5, 1979, installed on but not limited to the following aircraft," etc.)—and some mechanics, not knowing for sure when your particular magneto or vacuum pump (or whatever) was manufactured, will tear the unit down per the AD note *whether it needs it or not,* "just to be on the safe side." You can anticipate such situations (and bring them to a less costly conclusion) simply by reading AD notes yourself and making a phone call to the factory now and then to verify applicability requirements.

7. Unexpected engine work can make an annual inspection frustratingly expensive—and like it or not, such work is more apt to be needed on a high-time engine than a low-time one. The "500 hour" figure given in the question has no statistical significance; it was chosen merely to emphasize the fact that many of today's high-performance engines will go no longer than this without needing top-end work. (This is particularly true of the higher-horsepower Continental engines, which are very unforgiving of operator abuse.) Getting greater service life from pistons, rings, valves, valve guides, and other top-end components is mostly a matter of understanding—and catering to—your particular engine's special needs. The *average* operator of a high-performance aircraft engine can expect to be confronted with some kind of top-end work before 1,000 hours SMOH is reached. Be ready for it.

8. There is nothing inherently unhealthy about old age, either with people or with airplanes. It is certainly true, however, that the risk of finding structural cracks, airframe corrosion, and wear beyond limits in critical components increases with increasing airframe time. There is little one can do here except pray for the best as the plane is wheeled into the shop and the inspection covers come off for the 25th (30th? 40th? 100th?) time.

All of this, again, is by way of saying that there are some factors outside the pilot's control that can have a profound effect on the cost of an annual inspection, driving that cost up despite the operator's best efforts to economize. It is important for you to come to grips with these factors as they apply to your own aircraft. None of the cost-cutting techniques given here can make a run-out engine—or airframe, or magneto, or propeller—any younger.

STRATEGIES FOR SELECTION

Choosing a Shop: FBO vs. Clinic

Choosing the right maintenance facility is tremendously important for saving money on inspections. We have already seen how mere geography can influence shop rates dramatically. (It bears repeating that if you live in the southwest or northeast, you may well find it worth your while to fly a couple hundred miles east or south to have your annual done; the cost savings can be substantial.) But there is more to choosing a maintenance facility than studying a map.

What happens to your engine during the annual may well reflect what was done with and to it since the last annual. How well were its needs met?

The first question you should ask yourself is: "What kind of an nual do I want?" If you want (and have time) to participate in the inspection yourself, you will have to seek out a shop or an AI mechanic that specializes in this sort of thing—and not many do. We recommend that you go this route if at all possible, however, since it offers the best hope of saving several hundred dollars on an annual inspection. (Participating in your own annual will also, of course, teach you a great deal about your own plane's systems and maintenance requirements, enabling you to save money on repair work *throughout the year.*)

Participatory annuals—or "annual clinics"—have not yet become common in many parts of the country (although our reading of the situation is that such annuals *will* become much more popular and widely available over the next several years).

Operators who do specialize in "supervised annuals" do not necessarily advertise the fact, but they will open their hangars to do-it-yourselfers, say on evenings and weekends, charging a modest hourly fee for tool rental, hangar space, and consultation. After the customer preps the plane, the FBO will then do the "inspection" part of an annual inspection and will make all the appropriate log entries. If extra work is needed, he may show the aircraft owner how to go about accomplishing the work and how to obtain the necessary parts at the best possible price—or he may even welcome the owner's bringing his own parts.

The aircraft owner may be shown how to prep the airplane (remove all inspection covers, cowlings, etc.; drain the crankcase, replace the filter elements, and remove all the spark plugs; put the plane on jacks and pull the brake pads, wheels, and wheel bearings; and so forth) and then the AI will personally inspect everything that needs inspecting. The fee will probably depend on the type of aircraft and how much the AI must help the owner with the prep work.

As we said before, we strongly recommend that you go the "annual clinic" route if you can, since [1] you'll save hundreds of dollars by doing most of the labor yourself, and [2] you'll learn more about your plane and its maintenance requirements this way than you would in a year or two years of Saturday-afternoon tinkering. It's unfortunate that supervised annuals have not become common around the country (you may have to do quite a bit of looking around to find anything resembling an "annual clinic" in your part of the country)—but we believe that more and more shops will come around to the supervised-annual way of thinking in the near future, as the demands on AI-rated mechanics' time become more acute and as word gets out about the greater profitability (for shops and mechanics) of this kind of annual.

If you lack the time to participate in a supervised annual (or you cannot locate an "annual clinc" in your area), you will—of course—have to reach a decision on where to take your plane for a "normal" annual, and here, you'll have hundreds of shops to choose from. The question is, how do you go about choos-

The shop you commission to annual your plane should be experienced in working with the type. If, your Lake amphibian, say, is terra incognita but interesting to them, you too may have an "interesting" time in store.

ing the shop that will do the best job for the least amount of money?

Rule Number One: Select a shop that more or less specializes in repairing the type of airplane you have. (This immediately narrows the field considerably.) Do not make the mistake of taking your Mooney to a Cessna shop to be worked on. Nor should you consign your Cessna 402 to a shop that works mainly on single-engine planes. The same goes for taking an Aztec or a Lance to a Beech-oriented shop, taking a Baron to a Piper facility, etc.

If you give your Continental-powered Cessna over to a shop whose mechanics are used to working on Lycoming-powered Pipers, you'll not only end up paying for your plane's annual, but you'll also underwrite several man-hours (if not several man-days) of on-the-job training for those mechanics who've never worked on a Cessna P210 (or whatever) before. This is not a trivial concern, either; before a mechanic can begin work on a strange aircraft, he must (according to FAR 65.81) fully understand the "current instructions of the manufacturer, and the maintenance manuals, for the specific operation concerned.'' In other words, a mechanic may spend several hours reading the manufacturer's manuals before proceeding with various parts of the inspection—and someone has to pay for that man's reading time. (I.e., *you'll* have to pay for it.)

Another thing to consider when taking a Brand X airplane to a Brand Y shop—besides the possibility that you'll end up paying for somebody's on-the-job training—is the fact that mechanics (like pilots) are a prejudiced lot and tend to favor one aircraft type over another. This prejudice does not always run along strict dealer-affiliation lines, either. For instance, we know of one shop affiliated with a Cessna dealership whose mechanics enjoy working on Barons and Bonanzas most of all, take a dim view of most Cessna singles (particularly the 150 and 152), and absolutely abhor Mooneys. Theoretically, this shop's personnel should be most at home working on Cessna products . . . but in fact, the mechanics know more about Barons and Bonanzas than they do about any Cessna (by their own admission), and at least one senior mechanic in the shop has voiced a disliking for Lycoming engines. (''Too hard to work on,'' the man says.) Obviously, this is not the shop to take a brand new Mooney 201 to for an annual inspection.

Before deciding on a particular shop for your bird's annual inspection, talk with the mechanics. Ask what kinds of planes they work on the most. Attempt to get a feel, if you can, for their prejudices. If you can't talk to the mechanics directly, at least talk to some of the shop's regular customers—preferably those that own the same kind of plane that you own. (Are the customers happy? Have they ever had any complaints? How do customers rate this shop with others in the area?) If the shop is affiliated with an FBO that conducts air taxi operations—and the FBO operates Model X and Model Y planes as part of its air-taxi fleet—you can generally assume that the shop personnel are very knowledgeable regarding Model X and Y type aircraft. But that's about all you can safely assume. The shop hands may know little or nothing about Model Z aircraft (they may even dislike working on them) . . . even if the FBO in question is a Model Z dealer.

Other Considerations in Choosing a Shop

Getting a good deal on an annual inspection is largely a matter of seeking out a shop (or an individual AI mechanic) that specializes in working on just the kind of plane you own. It's also largely a matter of selecting a shop with reasonably low rates—and here, we don't mean flat rates so much as the basic hourly labor rate. (Almost all shops in the U.S. have gone to a "flat rate" system in which a flat fee is charged to cover the basic inspection and an hourly rate is added on to cover repairs not associated with the basic inspection. In other words, the owner of a Cessna 210 might be charged a flat-rate fee of $250 for all the labor associated with the basic inspection, *plus* an hour—or the shop's usual hourly rate—for "extra" repairs not covered by the flat-rate fee.) Comparison shopping should be done *first* on the basis of hourly shop rates, and *then* on the basis of flat-rate fee structures, for the simple reason that a small difference in hourly rates can quickly offset a large difference in flat rates between two shops, if "extra" repairs—or compliance with AD notes—are required. (Many FBOs, realizing full well that most pilots shop on the basis of flat rates rather than per-hour charges, deliberately set their flat rates low . . . then make up the difference with hefty hourly rates.) *Unless you're absolutely sure that your plane is up to date on all AD notes and can pass its annual squawk-free, you're generally better off choosing the shop with the lower hourly rate, even if that shop's flat rates are high.*

This is not to say that you shouldn't pay any attention at all to flat rates—you should. (By all means *do* get flat-rate quotes from various shops, along with quotes for per-hour labor rates.) Just be sure that when you compare flat rate fees, you do it on an "apples to apples" basis. That is: When you ask about a shop's flat rates, find out exactly what the basic flat-rate fee includes. Does it include hangar storage for the duration of the annual? (Many shops charge an extra $4 or $5 a day for storage . . . over and above the basic inspection fee.) Does it include oil and filter changes performed in conjunction with the inspection? (Again, many shops charge extra for both the parts *and labor* involved in oil and filter changes. Some charge extra for just the parts.) Does it include a logbook sign-off by an Inspection-Authorized A&P—or does the inspector get an additional fee? (It's not uncommon—in the U.S., at least—for the inspecting mechanic to tack an additional $50 onto the basic flat-rate charge, as his personal "inspection fee.")

From the foregoing, it should be obvious that there's no way a plane-owner can tell which of five different shops is "cheapest" simply on the basis of comparing five flat-rate fees quoted out of context. (The "cheapest" shop may or may not be the least expensive. It depends on exactly what the flat-rate fees cover.) You have to compare apples to apples. And unfortunately, the real world is fruit cocktail.

How to Protect Yourself Against Fraud

Recent studies indicate that as much as 40 percent of the money spent in the U.S. on automobile repairs is wasted. Experts attribute approximately one-half of the waste to ineptitude on the part of maintenance personnel and approximately half to fraud. We expect that the corresponding figures for general aviation maintenance (if there *were* any corresponding figures, which there aren't—yet) would be quite a bit less, due to the higher standards (for education and for on-the-job performance) set for aircraft maintenance personnel. Nonetheless, a certain amount of less-than-honorable repair work does go on in general aviation. Thus, for your own protection,

Busy mechanic at work: How knowledgeable is he? How efficient, honest? How much specific interest will he permit you to take in his work on your airplane? Before committing yourself, if in doubt pull out.

we must advise you to adhere unwaveringly to the following guidelines when choosing a shop to perform an annual inspection:

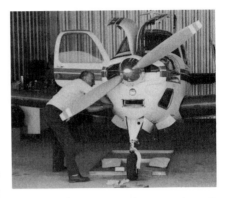

1. *Don't do business with any establishment that will not agree to consult with you before undertaking expensive repairs.* Leave your phone number and insist that you be notified prior to any major squawks being worked off. (Tell them you consider anything costing more than $25 to be "major".)

2. *Don't do business with any repair facility that will not agree to present you with any old parts that are replaced during the inspection.* This precaution, admittedly, is not 100-percent

Prepping for an annual means that all cowls, fairings, and inspection covers must come off, the spark plugs must be pulled, the fuel-system screens taken out, the air and oil filters removed, the battery lifted from its box, the muffler shroud unbuttoned, and (in many cases) the plane's seats taken out. But if you can arrange to do the "prep" work yourself, the rewards should be substantial—money-wise and knowledge-wise.

foolproof—any large shop can dig up enough "trash can" parts from previous jobs to convince you that *your* spark plugs (or brake linings, or whatever) were "totally shot"—but it's a precaution worth taking nonetheless. A legitimate, "above-board" shop will not back away from a request to produce old parts replaced during the inspection.

3. *Don't patronize any repair shop that refuses to allow the customer to specify the brands and names of replacement parts to be used.* If you want AC spark plugs instead of Champions, or a Wall Colmonoy Nicrocraft muffler instead of a Cessna or Beech or Piper muffler, or a Superior Air Parts cylinder assembly instead of a Teledyne Continental assembly, that should be your right as a customer. (After all, you're paying the money.) If the shop doesn't want the customer deciding what parts to buy, go elsewhere.

In addition to observing the foregoing rules (which we consider hard-and-fast), we urge you not to do business with any shop that won't let you stand by and watch as the inspection is performed.

(This suggestion is not hard-and-fast, however, since we recognize that not all shops that don't want pilots hanging around are dishonest.) Some shops, of course, have liability insurance of the kind that prohibits non-employees from remaining in the workplace. In that case, offer to sign a "hold harmless" agreement. We feel very strongly that the aircraft owner should be allowed to at least *observe* (if not participate in) the annual inspection, both to protect him/herself against dishonest maintenance practices and to verify that the plane's systems are, in fact, airworthy. If it is necessary for you to fly an extra 100 miles out of your way (and perhaps pay an extra $100) in order for you to be present when the annual inspection is conducted, we recommend that you fly the 100 miles (and pay the $100).

We are not 100-percent conviced that mandatory "safety" inspections (for cars *or* airplanes) are actually worthwhile. They are certainly no guarantee of safety. Engines still catch fire, controls are improperly rigged, tires and spark plugs fail, etc., the day after the inspection. We've seen it happen too many times.

There is, in fact, we think, the very real possibility that mandatory periodic inspections—by exposing a machine's systems to so many sets of probing hands (whether the systems *need* to be probed or not)—actually result in the creation of *new* safety hazards. We saw graphic evidence for this in May 1979 at O'Hare International, when a thoroughly inspected and safety-certified "no squawks" engine flew off a fully loaded DC-10. (Here, the requirement for periodic removal and inspection of the aircraft's engines had resulted in the "invention" of an entirely new and unexpected failure mode.) One need not look to DC-10's to find inspection-related damage, however. We see it all the time on general aviation aircraft.

Whether or not the mandatory laying on of hands actually increases air safety is, to say the least, a debatable point. There can be no debate, however, regarding the fact that mandatory inspections—by virtue of their mandatoriness—result inevitably in the wasting of many, many dollars. (And shillings, and Deutsche marks, and rupiah.) The mandatory nature of "safety" inspections destroys competition, encourages price-fixing (and -gouging), and promotes corruption. (Anywhere in the U.S., you can buy a "rubber-stamp" inspection—for your car *or* plane—almost as easily as you can buy a carton of potato salad. Many a used aircraft in this country is in fact, sold with a "rubber stamp" annual inspection.)

We believe that the safety risks posed by the over-inspection of aircraft systems, the inappropriateness of having one set of rules to cover all types of aircraft (Cessna 150's and light twins, aircraft that are flown 500 hours a year and aircraft that fly just 5 hours a year, etc.), the inefficiency of annual inspections in detecting incipient engine problems, the increasingly outrageous *cost* of annual inspections, and the remarkable improvement in the reliability of aircraft systems that's taken place in the 20 years or so since our periodic-inspection regulations were last rewritten . . . all speak to the need for a complete overhaul (or at least a serious reconsideration) of our present periodic-inspection regulations.

Until such an overhaul is undertaken, annual inspections will no doubt continue to figure heavily in every plane-owner's annual maintenance budget. Just how heavily, though, is up to you. By choosing a shop that specializes in inspecting your type of aircraft . . . by participating in your own annual as much as you can . . . by correcting minor squawks yourself before wheeling the plane into the shop . . . by reading the AD notes yourself, beforehand, to see if they're really applicable to your plane . . . and by selecting a shop with low *hourly* rates (and a good reputation among local pilots)—to name just a few of the techniques covered here—you ought to be able to save hundreds (perhaps thousands) of dollars on annual inspections over the coming years.

Annual inspections may, like death and taxes, be here to stay . . . but that doesn't mean you must kneel in submission when the Grim Reaper comes to collect. We prefer to stand tall . . . .and cover our pockets.

THE PRE-ANNUAL INSPECTION

Since the object of the annual-inspection exercise for the belabored owner is to go through it with the best service for the least outlay, he will be wise to resort to such defenses against unnecessary expenditure as sagacious shopping and even becoming a working part of the inspection process. Laying hands on his own plane during the annual can trim labor and parts costs—assuming that the chosen IA/A&P will let him.

As we have seen, therein may lie a problem, for not all shops are enlightened enough to encourage or even allow "participatory annuals," profitable though they may be. Furthermore, not all owners are on good enough terms with (and live close enough to a willing) IA/A&P or can spare the necessary 20 to 50 person-hours of labor to do an owner-assisted annual.

If the participatory route is closed to you, the next-best way to economize on annuals is to conduct your own pre-annual inspections some two to six weeks before your plane is scheduled to go into the shop.

The purpose of the pre-annual inspection is simply to discover (and, if possible, fix cheaply) whatever squawks your plane has, yourself, before handing it over to a mechanic. By spotting and correcting minor defects yourself, you come out ahead two ways. First, you save money (fistfuls of it) on *parts*, since you're free, at this stage, to go out and buy whatever replacements you need from discount parts suppliers. (You can buy new spark plugs now at 40-percent off . . . or you can wait two weeks and let your FBO charge you full retail. Likewise, you can add less than a dollar's worth of hydraulic fluid to your reservoir now . . . or face a multidollar brake-fluid surcharge later. The choice is yours.) Second, you save money on *labor*—if you don't mind donating a few hours on a Saturday morning to doing a little of your own fix-it work. (Even if your time is worth more than the hourly rate you'll pay to have someone else poke around under the cowl, you owe it to yourself to spend at least a few hours a year getting to know your engine, brakes, controls, etc. on a firsthand basis.)

The Golden Discount Factor

Just to illustrate the kind of savings we're talking about, let us suppose you put your plane—a late-model Cessna or Beech, say—in the shop . . . only to be told, a few days later, that you need a new battery. If you're doing business with a Cessna or Beech dealer, the chief mechanic will assume that you want to replace your plane's battery—a 24-volt Gill PS12-11—-with a new one just like it. After putting your new battery on the shop charger (hook-up fee), the mechanic cleans your battery box and installs the new battery (20 minutes' labor at the going rate), later adding the retail list price of the battery plus applicable sales tax to your final bill. Adding it up,

If you bring to the annual an airplane that clearly has been well maintained by a savvy owner, both you and the machine are more likely to be treated with the honesty you deserve.

your bill for installation of the new battery comes to nearly $300—not including local taxes.

Now suppose you had discovered the weak battery yourself during a cursory, last-minute pre-annual inspection. Is the battery truly dead? You take it home and put it on the charger overnight. It won't take a charge. Therefore, you decide to order a new battery. At this point, if you were buying a 12-volter, you'd be free to choose between any of a half dozen quality brands of aircraft batteries, which you can obtain at discounts from zero to 52 percent from any number of suppliers listed in *Trade-A-Plane* and elsewhere; you're *not* forced to buy a Gill battery (*the* most expensive battery on the market) from your local FBO. But if, as we have supposed in the foregoing example, your plane is a late-model Cessna or Beech with a 24-volt battery, you probably will buy a Gill replacement. Even so, you don't have to pay full retail; instead, you can get your PS12-11 (brand new, with electrolyte) at a discount savings of 36 percent off the manufacturer's suggested retail. Instead of sales tax, you pay

UPS shipping. And instead of a hook-up fee, you activate the battery on your own charger at home and pay nothing for installation. By doing the work yourself, you end up getting a new 24-volt Gill battery for a total cost of more than $100 *less* than you would have paid to have the same battery installed in the course of an annual inspection. (Even if you were to have to go out and buy your own 24-volt charger, you'd *still* save overall by replacing the battery yourself.)

Proper Timing Is the Key

Obviously, it doesn't take many $100 squawks of this kind to add up to several hundred dollars in potential savings when annual-inspection time rolls around. But the point is that in order for you to reap those savings, *you have to take time to perform your own pre-annual inspection.* Once the plane is in the shop, it's too late—it's out of your hands.

Naturally, how thorough your pre-annual inspections should be will depend partly on how well you've maintained your plane throughout the year. (If you installed a new battery two months back, your tires are new, and your plugs have been cleaned and rotated on a strict 25-hour schedule, those particular items don't warrant special attention during your pre-annual inspection.) The thoroughness of your pre-annual should also depend on how intimately familiar *you* are with the *actual* state of health of your plane's systems and sub-systems—as opposed to the picture of health conveyed by the copious scribblings of A&Ps in your logbooks (which, for all you know, could be phony). Have you been doublechecking your mechanic's work all year? If not, be thorough in your pre-annual inspection. Don't merely take logbook entries at face value.

Plan on beginning your pre-annual inspection a full month, if possible, before your next scheduled inspection. That way, you'll have more than sufficient time to order discount parts (tires, batteries, spark plugs, filters, etc.) by mail or UPS, and install them yourself, before the "real" inspection.

Depending on what your personal schedule is like, you may wish to perform your pre-annual inspection progressively, over two or three weekends, noting minor squawks (and what parts to order) at first, then fixing those squawks in later sessions. Ideally, you should use a checklist—the 100-hour or annual-inspection checklist that comes in the service manual for your aircraft. The idea is simply to go down the items in this checklist, checking everything you can easily check yourself, and fixing (or ordering parts for) anything that needs fixing. Naturally, you'll want to check not only such high-wear items as tires, brake linings, and spark plugs, but also such less-obvious potential trouble areas as ELT batteries, lamps and bulbs, seat belts (which must be of the metal-to-metal latch kind), vacuum filters, oleo struts, control system pulleys, etc.

If any of the two or three hundred screws holding down your plane's nonstructural cover plates, cowls, and/or fairings are rusted up (and they will be, if you're using standard cadmium-plated steel hardware), now's a good time to remove those fasteners and replace them with rustproof stainless-steel equivalents. As any mechanic will tell you, much of the labor involved in any annual inspection centers around the removal and replacement of those hundreds of tiny screws, scores of which won't come out without the use of vast quantities of LPS-1 or WD40, and some of which will not be loosened even then. (Badly rusted screws will have to be drilled out.) Better to replace some of those screws yourself, now, than to pay by the hour to have them replaced later.

False Alarms and Unnecessary Costs

Be on the lookout for new fuel stains—indicating possible leaks *or* (just as possible) normal seepage—as you inspect your plane. Note the locations and severity of any stain(s) you find—then eradicate them with degreaser and/or Stoddard solvent. If the stains reappear, along with a fuel odor, a few weeks later (at the normal inspection time), you'll know you've got a legitimate fuel leak which should be corrected. If the cleaned-up stains do *not* reappear, you've saved yourself a potentially expensive repair job on a fuel cell, fuel selector valve, or whatever, because now your mechanic cannot point his finger at a perfectly harmless stain indicating normal seepage and say "Aha! A dangerous fuel leak!"

Unless you're a fanatic about such things, there's no reason to take your muffler off, weeks before the actual annual, and peer into it to see if any baffles are broken—your mechanic will do this at no extra charge when the time comes. If you suspect broken baffles are blocking the muffler outlet, however (as indicated by intermittently poor takeoff power or static rpm, occasional poor climb performance, and other strange symptoms), remove the shroud from your muffler and knock the bottom of the unit firmly with a rubber mallet. If the muffler contains broken baffles, you'll hear them jangle around. (The thing to do then is to send the unit off for repair or order a rebuilt Nicroflite replacement muffler. You'll save tens, maybe *hundreds*, of dollars ordering mufflers from discount suppliers compared to buying new replacements from Cessna, Piper, or Beech.)

FBO's and IA mechanics are famous for making aircraft owners buy new ELT batteries at full retail prices, whether the ''new'' batteries have the full shelf life left in them or not. You might as will buy a discount battery now and install it yourself; the installation job is simple, and 100-percent legal for pilot-owners.

Of course, if you *really* want to save money on ELT upkeep, just take the thing out of the airplane and hang a placard stating ''ELT not installed'' in view of the pilot. When your mechanic asks you about this, refer him to FAR 91.52(f) (10). That should settle the matter to his and your satisfaction.

It is not necessary for you to pull and inspect wheel bearings as part of your pre-annual inspections, nor should you waste time performing any kind of lubrication. These operations will be performed at no extra cost during the actual annual inspection.

By the same token, because an oil change is part of what you get when you pay for an annual inspection, it makes no sense to change oil yourself, just before taking the bird to the shop. Rather, leave this potentially messy job to the mechanics. If, as is often the case, the actual cost of the *oil itself* (and/or filter elements) is not included in the ''flat rate'' fee for the inspection, it may pay you to go out and buy your own discounted oil and/or filters, and bring them with you when you wheel the plane into the shop. (Try to time your flying so that your next scheduled oil change coincides with the date of the annual inspection.) If your shop looks down on the practice of pilots bringing their own oil and supplies to an annual inspection along with the airplane, do business with a different shop.

A word to the wise: Don't bring your plane into the shop ''dirty.'' Clean the dirt from your windows, wipe the soot off your oleo struts, remove any traces of oil from your prop and engine (exterior) . . . in general, *clean up your plane* before you take it in for its annual

The only way you can know for sure that your spark plugs need not be replaced or regapped during the annual is to pull and service them yourself just before the inspection. If you do need new ones, buy at discount beforehand.

inspection. Mechanics, being only human, often tend to sum a plane up on the basis of first impressions. If fluid is oozing visibly from the oleos, the engine compartment is lettered with bits of birds' nests, the prop is oily, the cowl is exhaust-stained, and two of the planes's tires are about flat, your mechanic is going to take one look at your plane and mutter to himself: ''Jeez, what a sorry-looking piece of machinery. This thing's in bad shape!'' As a result, you just may get a more thorough annual inspection than you bargained for . . . even though the plane is basically sound. (Conversely, if you wheel the plane into the hangar all bright and shiny, tires full of air, the mechanic's natural tendency is to think: ''Hmm, this baby's obviously been kept up.'')

Once you've given your plane a thorough pre-annual check-up, you'll have a good idea where you stand going into the actual annual. You'll know precisely what your plane's strong points are. (If you have just changed spark plugs and battery, for example, you can be sure the mechanics will find no legitimate squawks in *those* areas.) Just as important, you'll know precisely what your plane's *weak* points are. One of the by-products of your pre-annual inspection will be (or should be) a detailed *squawk list* that you can hand over to your mechanics as they wheel your bird into the shop. On this list will be all the things that need fixing, but that you don't have time to (or can't legally) fix yourself. *Do* bring a squawk list with you. *Don't* assume that the mechanics will automatically stumble onto those discrepancies, such as a weak brake pedal or a control wheel with too much slack, that you feel should be corrected. (You'd be surprised at the things that go undetected and uncorrected at annual-inspection time.)

Pre-annual inspections are good for everybody—because they help take the guesswork out of the inspection process, eliminating last-minute major surprises. There may be a better way to save money on annuals than to go over the plane yourself, clipboard and torque wrench in hand, inventorying the plane's strong and weak points, and correcting the latter (as inexpensively as possible) yourself, well in advance of the actual Day of Inspection . . . but if there is, we haven't heard it.

THE POST-ANNUAL LIFESAVER

Ask any oldtimer, and you'll get the same story: If there is one time more than any other when mechanical mayhem is likely to manifest itself in an airplane, it is immediately following an annual inspection. No truly prudent pilot would plan a hard-IFR flight in the first hours after an annual, and any VFR pilot would be smart in similarly adopting a check-first-then-fly iron rule. The reasons why

After the inspection, examine the engine compartment and other sections for tools, debris, and various oddities left where they can cause disruption.

On many aircraft, the tailcone-to-rudder clearance is so slim that poor reinstallation of a tail stinger can cause rudder binding. Check for this after any annual or handling by a mechanic.

are as numerous as the parts of a plane an inspecting mechanic can touch.

On just one airplane, a Cessna 182, we have seen such post-annual phenomena as cowl flaps (formerly operable) that wouldn't close, rudders (formerly working) that would bind, dragging brakes, inspection panels left off, prop spinners installed 180 degrees reversed, tools left under floor boards, oil-temp and CHT probes damaged during inspection, and frozen pulleys that obviously weren't even checked for freedom—all this in just one airplane. We have made a post-annual engine startup in that 182, our flagship, only to have a three-foot screwdriver fall out from behind the instrument panel!

On the Skylane's second annual, we learned that a three-year old magneto AD had never been complied with. (It could have been serious; the impulse coupling flyweights on both mags were in fact ready to drop down into the back of the engine.)

On another occasion, we got the 182 back from an annual with a huge (thumbnail-sized) gouge in the prop—a *brand-new* gouge, at the most critical possible leading edge station, about 10 inches from the tip. That, plus a rough (very rough) magneto—No Extra Charge.

These experiences (and others like them) convince us of the wisdom of an owner's getting personally involved in the annual-inspection process—a tactic *LPM* has championed for years.

Not every operator has the time or wherewithal to go the participatory-annual route. But every operator *does* have the duty (under FAR 91.29 and 91.163) to see that his or her aircraft is in airworthy condition before each flight; and regulations or no regulations, the truly prudent operator will insist on a post-inspection inspection of any plane that has still-wet ink in the maintenance logs.

If you do nothing else, at least check for potentially life-threatening snafus: ailerons rigged backwards, controls binding, trim tabs reversed (Beech products especially), loose hardware in the engine intake duct, three-foot screwdrivers behind the instrument panel—that sort of thing.

Another thing you can do is check out anything your mechanics say they've "fixed." (You did get a squawk sheet with the annual, didn't you?) Be sure oil filters and drain bolts are safetied—we've seen some that weren't—and if you have time, ask Mr. Goodwrench point-blank whether the engine was run *after* the oil change and exactly what checks were done during that runup. (Was idle mixture checked? Oil pressure? Mags? Fuel flow? FAR 43.15 *requires* an engine run, and checks of certain items.) If the engine was run and observed for oil leaks, this fact should be clearly stated in the maintenance records. If it's not there, ask your mechanic about it.

Were all the inspection panels (and screws) returned to your airplane after the inspection? It's nothing new, of course, for so-called "meticulous" mechanics to replace stainless-steel screws with cheap cad-plated junk in the course of an inspection (it's the rare shop that does the reverse), but planes do occasionally come out of the shop missing entire panels. We know, because our freshly annualed 182 was delivered to us minus the trim-actuator inspection plate under the right horizontal stabilizer. (No explanation was given.) Since a horizontal stabilizer acts like an upside-down wing—generating lift in a *downward* direction in flight—a gaping six-inch hole in the bottom of a horizontal stabilizer is like having a two-foot opening in the top skin of one wing. It can't do the airplane any good.

In general, any fairing, inspection panel, or bulkhead that can be reinstalled incorrectly ought to be given a look-see before you taxi into position for takeoff. For many aircraft, that includes the tail stinger. We once got the Lane back with the tail stinger installed so badly out of whack that the rudder knocked against it. (The clearance is normally only .250 to .500 inch to begin with.) Cowlings and cooling baffles are also worth checking, as most AIs let their minimum-wage gofers reinstall these items, rather than do it themselves. On the Cessna 310, it's possible to install the left top cowl half on the right engine, and the right top cowl half on the left engine, creating air gaps big enough to poke fourth-class mail through. We didn't know this was possible until some otherwise-fine mechanics kindly did this to our airplane.

A corollary to the above: Check to be sure that anything that can possibly be installed *backwards* (or 180 degrees reversed) hasn't been. This includes

Crucial items to check forward of the firewall: [1] the carb/injector screen lock-washers; [2] the sump plug safety-wire; [3] proper safetying of the oil filter; [4] the tightness of the skat tubing clamps; [5] the security of the air-box. They have life-and-death status.

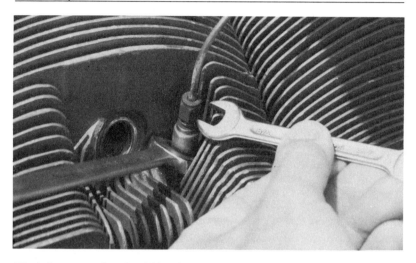

The injector nozzles should be cleaned during the annual, but often they are not. Check this during the post-annual.

prop spinners on two-bladed aircraft, trim tabs on Barons, Travel Airs, and Bonanzas, and a variety of symmetrical items on other aircraft. A Queen Air gear-collapse incident occurred because a nut was reinstalled 180 degrees out of phase on a gear actuator. Most bolts are single-threaded, but the Queen Air actuator uses a double-acme-threaded nut which can be started in either of two positions, 180 degrees apart. The appropriate maintenance procedure is to mark (or index) the nut and shank on disassembly, so that on reassembly the same thread engagement is used. (Each thread cut can have its own unique surface features. After ''seating'' in one orientation, the nut and shank threads should never be engaged in the opposite pattern, or else rapid wear may occur.) This is discussed in the Beech Model 80 maintenance manual, but apparently some mechanics are not getting the message, since the above mistake has felled more than one Queen Air.

Based on foulups, bleeps, and blunders we've actually seen happen, our own post-annual inspection checklist includes the following:

1. Airframe exterior: Check for missing screws, panels, inspection plates. (Get on your knees and check the underside of the aircraft;

look for rags in the wheel wells, etc.) Check the fairings, prop spinner, tail stinger. Remove mechanics' fingerprints with Fantastik.

2. Airframe interior: Check the tailcone, floor, and intrument panel for loose tools. Also check for screws missing from upholstery panels, fuel selectors turned off. In some aircraft, like the 310, the gear system won't work if the emergency crank isn't stowed properly. So check the gear emergency lowering system for proper configuration.

During the annual, most old oil filters are simply thrown away rather than opened.

3. Controls: Check for friction, odd noises, improper operation. Check for full travel range of controls, including electric trim (if applicable). Be sure the engine controls have the proper amount of ''cushion'' before hitting the panel. If the carb heat or alternate air knobs actually *hit* the panel, you don't know for sure whether the air valve is fully shut ahead of the firewall. The same principle applies to mixture, prop, and throttle as well.

4. Cabin: Have the seat stops been reinstalled properly? Does the door latch? Do the air vents work? Is anything broken?

5. Engine compartment: Check that the cowling has been installed properly. If possible, remove the cowling and check the security of the ignition wires, cooling baffles, airbox-to-carburetor connections, air filter security, magneto security, etc. Look for loose tools lying between cylinder fins. Investigate fuel or oil spills. Visually confirm dryness of oil filter base, sump drain bolt, and oil cooler connections, and check for the presence of safety wire on filters and drain points. (Filters should be wired to the adaptor, by the way, and not random points in the engine compartment.) Wiggle the P-leads and oil filler cap. Check the carburetor bowl drain plug and inlet screen plug to see if they've been serviced, and if so, whether they've been safetied (with wire in the bowl plug; bent-tab lock washer under in-

let screen hex). Finally, pull the dipstick and confirm the presence of oil in the sump.

6. Lube points: You'll be surprised what you might see when you begin checking rod ends, clevises, and zerk fittings. Expect to find a lot of them bone-dry or frozen solid. Zerk fittings should at least look like they've seen grease, but don't let initial appearances fool you. We've seen closed-off grease nipples—grease fittings that were obviously *painted over* during previous paint

Check the grease fittings, which may or may not get a proper greasing in the shop, for thorough lubing..

jobs—get a fruitless "greasing" by inexperienced mechanics during 100-hour inspections (time after time), with nobody taking time to first scrape the paint off the fittings' openings.

7. Landing gear: Exercise the brakes. Check for new hydraulic leaks. Wipe the oleos clean. Examine the zerk fittings (see above).

8. Electrical: Be sure all circuit breakers and fuses have been reset before you attempt to fly the airplane. A Cessna Citation crashed at the factory when thrust reversers deployed just after takeoff. (No one was killed, luckily.) Cessna mechanics had pulled the plane's thrust-reverse circuit breakers during maintenance and forgot to push them back in when work was finished. The engine's clam-shells were flush but not locked in the stowed position; so they passed the preflight inspection. On takeoff, they flapped open in the breeze, deploying in the slipstream.

9. Propeller: Examine for new nicks, improperly dressed edges, improperly installed spinner or bulkhead.

10. Miscellaneous: If you can, do a spot check of the control-system pulleys. We've noticed that frozen pulleys often go undetected for years, during which time flat spots are worn into the phenolic sheaves (reducing cable tension and giving controls a "sloppy" feel). Many of today's younger mechanics are simply not in the habit of rotating the pulleys so that flat spots are "evened

out." If you find a stuck pulley, free it with LPS 1, Mouse Milk, WD-40, or equivalent, and *rotate the pulley 180 degrees* so as to bring the "unused side" up. If the pulley is badly flat-spotted, it will eventually rotate back to the "good-side-down" orientation in service. If this is what you find on subsequent inspections, arrange to have the errant pulley replaced.

In the end, the best checklist to use for the post-annual inspection may well be the one your mechanics used for the annual itself. (FARs require mechanics to use a checklist, by the way, during the performance of any 100-hour or annual inspection. You might quiz your mechanics on exactly what kind of checklist they used. We've seen shops use Cessna checklists to annual Mooneys, Piper checklists to inspect Cessnas, etc.) The ideal thing to do would be to go through the entire annual inspection checklist yourself—but of course then you'd be doing your own annual inspection. Which is what we've been recommending for years.

As we say, if you do nothing else, *at least* check safety-of-flight items. All the hull insurance in the world isn't worth a thing when you're sitting upside-down in a tree with 100LL dripping on your face.

Chapter 7

RIGGING AND OTHER CRITICAL EXAMINATIONS

The annual inspection mercifully occurs relatively infrequently, but the need and responsibility for keeping the health of your airplane carefully monitored and in excellent condition is never ending, as many an accident has borne out. Every preflight should be performed to professional standards.

Yet not all preflights are equal. Particularly critical is the highly detailed one you should perform whenever you prepare to take up an airplane that has been grounded awhile. Like a summer athlete who has sat out the winter, an airplane may come out of inactivity stiff, rusty, and perhaps ailing. Aloft is no place to discover how far out of shape it has fallen. We will open this chapter, therefore, by describing how you can determine how ready to fly your airplane actually is.

The bulk of the chapter concerns checks and procedures for proper rigging. Every aircraft sends its pilot signals about how comfortable it is in responding to the forces it encounters in flight. Often, these messages pertain to how adequately the craft is rigged. The truly proficient owner-pilot learns to detect and interpret these signals and sees that any faults are corrected. He knows that to sense how well his aircraft is rigged is to touch its very personality.

The checks in this chapter, therefore, are easily as important to safety and flying comfort as those of any annual.

THE POST-INACTIVITY INSPECTION

Many pilots have trouble getting as much flight out of their aircraft as they would like. This is especially true for, but not limited to, the winter months. If your plane has been grounded in the snow or by other winter conditions or, for that matter, by discouraging circumstances during any season, you should perform a *50-hour* inspection. This is no mere walk-around preflight performed with more piercing looks than usual but a super-thorough examination by the pilot. Making such an inspection every 50 hours—or at least before that first flight after a long layoff—could save your airframe, your powerplant, or your life.

Before attempting anything else, remove the battery, check its fluid, wash off its top and clean and dress the terminals. Then check the vent lines for crimping or blockage. If you have a trickle charger (not over five amps), run a charge on it for a few hours or overnight; most of the following steps can be completed without the battery in the airplane.

Add air to the tires (because of the characteristics of aircraft tubes, they are bound to be low) and service the struts. Cold weather and idleness allow oleo strut seals to dry out or leak. Time not in motion is one of the cruelest punishments for mechanical devices that are supposed to fly.

The Crucial Wash

Next, wash the airplane. This is not just a once-over, but some-

A plane left out and unflown in winter need not have languished in deep snow drifts to warrant a close and wary spring first preflight.

thing necessary to the greater scheme of things. Start by purchasing two, possibly three, aerosol cans of Gunk engine cleanser. Remove the upper cowling and spray down the engine and firewall area as best you can with the Gunk (on some aircraft, to do a decent job, removal of the lower cowling will also be necessary). Avoid spraying the vacuum pump and any openings in alternators or starters or other accessories. Expect to use a little over one can of Gunk on the engine and firewall. Then, while the Gunk is working, use the balance of the second can on the belly, and on the landing gear, brakes and control

Oleo struts that have gone flat can cause deep trouble if they are not attended to prior to taxi.

hinges. Unless (through carelessness) you absolutely saturate the brake pucks, the Gunk—which has an emulsifier mixed with its solvent—will wash off nicely with water. After fifteen minutes or so, go ahead and flush the engine and belly with lots of water (hot, if available, but don't use a high pressure spray).

Attack any remaining oil or exhaust stains with Formula 409, diluted 50/50 with water, which does a nice job of removing grime. (Such cleansers are demonstrably harsher on paint than is Gunk, so it may be prudent to test them first in an inconspicuous area.) Use full strength 409 and old toothbrushes to clean the landing gear and brakes. Hose down these items thoroughly and frequently before the 409 dries.

If your airplane has a low wing, move it to a drier spot before completing the wash job, so you can wash the belly without lying in pools of water and muck. Wash the belly and the bottoms of the wings first, before doing the upper fuselage and the wings' upper surfaces. Use a car washing liquid such as the one by Turtle Wax.

Such products are easier on paint than liquid dish detergents and products used in the laundry. (Why worry about these things after just attacking the paint with solvent and 409? Because powerful cleansers are necessary to degrease the belly, unless you do it very frequently. But overall, there is no need to escalate your weaponry any more than is absolutely necessary.) Pay particular concern to removing biological debris (bugs) from the leading edges of the wings and other surfaces, as the acids in insect carcasses are very hard on paint. (If at all possible, bug stains should be removed in the fall and should not be permitted to remain until spring.) Rinse the airframe thoroughly working from the aft end forward, so you can wash out any solvents and detergents that seep into the gaps in the lapped skins.

During the washing process, take the opportunity to check the skin for surface corrosion or flaking areas of paint. If water breaks through the paint at a chip or skin lap, the constant freezing and thawing process of winter, fall and spring will literally peel away whole areas of paint. Earmark chipped areas for later touch up. Check the exposed surfaces of any control cables, hardware or pushrods for signs of corrosion; be very wary of corroded control cables and hardware. Control pushrods are often of 4130 steel with rod ends at each end. If the paint is gone or chipped, this must be corrected, preferably long before annual time. If you discover control cable, pushrod, or hardware corrosion, ask your mechanic for advice.

Watch for signs of fuel or fluid leaks. Often, you will find gummy green (or red, if you can still get 80 octane) deposits at the wing roots. This demands further investigation. By removing wing root fairings, you may find that such apparent fuel leaks can be cured by tightening the Adel clamps that commonly hook the tank nipples to the fuel lines. The other common source of such stains, of course, is quick drains. Their leaks can almost always be cured by draining the tank and then removing the quick drains and replacing their O-rings. At any rate, clean off the fuel dye stains carefully, from both sides of the wing root fairings if they are so affected. That way, a potential problem area is ready to be watched carefully. For example, should you note a bit of seepage when your tanks are full, you will be forced to consider new bladders if this develops as a problem.

Cleaning the aircraft is at the very crux of this preflight activity. It has little to do with cosmetics, so we are not going to tell you how to clean the windshield or suggest vacuuming the interior, unless you haul goats for a hobby. Here's why the exterior cleaning process is so important:

First, flooding the airframe with water presents a perfect opportunity to check the cabin and cockpit door seals for new water leaks. (Open all these doors and investigate while you are waiting for the airplane to dry.) Secondly, it forces you to look at each square inch of the airplane, and exposes the bare surface so you can inspect for various fluid leaks. If you read the FAA regs carefully, you will discover that a mechanic is not supposed to begin an inspection without thoroughly cleaning the components of an aircraft or its powerplant. There are good reasons for this.

Controls Checks and Runup

Your next step, after washing, should be to check all hydraulic and brake fluid reservoirs and other fluids, such as for retractable landing gear hydraulic pumps for proper quantity. Then, climb into the pilot's seat and lean on the brakes. Heavily. Not once, but several times. Hold them firmly for a half minute. Then jump out and check each main wheel and brake assembly, and all visible lines for the telltale red color of hydraulic fluid. While you are at each wheel, wiggle any flexible pressure lines, and inspect them for fraying. Such lines should be replaced every five years or so; left untended, they can actually get quite brittle. The consequences are obvious.

Before recowling the engine, reinstall the charged battery and also install a knowledgeable assistant in the captain's seat. With that person working each control throughout its range while you watch at its opposite end, watch and listen for any indication of friction, binding, security of attachment hardware, and even outright fatigue breaks. In short, do a functional check on each control, instrument and system. Move the throttle through its full travel; do the same for prop, mixture, carburetor heat, and all the cabin heat and vent controls. Move the flight controls and trim handles throughout their complete range. Don't be afraid to squirt oil or WD-40 on moving or bearing surfaces. Turn on, or have turned on, all lighting systems while you visually check them for operating condition. Check the travel of the cowl flaps, making certain they close completely. Vibration is one of an aircraft's worst enemies; with reciprocating powerplants, vibration is necessarily concentrated in the vicinity of the engine. Wiggle, stretch, and visually inspect each bit of cable and hardware and other devices forward of the firewall.

If the tail is tied down and the aircraft securely chocked, pull the prop through numerous times, slowly, with the magnetos off. (Be careful, please. Forego this step if you don't know what you are doing.) The compression on each cylinder should feel similar; if you can stop on top dead center, your assistant can listen at the exhaust

Flexible brake lines should be inspected for deterioration and leaks.

stack for possible exhaust valve leaks. Realize that the walls of your cylinders are probably dry, so that this is not a critical test of compression. What you are looking for is a dead cylinder due to a stuck valve; do this test after shut-down for a more valid assessment of the engine's condition.

With the strainers drained and oil above minimum capacity, and after inspecting such things as exhaust stud nuts and the other items illustrated in the accompanying photographs, recowl and start the engine. Expect most engines that have been idle to clank for a while, due to bled down hydraulic lifters; check the oil pressure immediately. Allow the engine to warm to operating temperature, and taxi out to a spot where you can do a runup at full power without being a nuisance or subjecting your prop to gravel chips. Leave the cowl flaps open at all items on the ground, despite what you have heard to the contrary; closing the cowl flaps to accelerate warm-up subjects the cylinders to localized overheating. While you are taxiing, functionally test the flight instruments by doing some S-turns, and ride the brakes a bit to clean corrosion off the brake disks. If enough navigational aids are available on the surface, turn on each, and all, of your avionics for a functional test, including dual or VOT tests for the omnis. The ADF can be tested for proper swing while S-turning.

Probing Firewall-Forward

Once your runup is complete, return to the ramp and uncowl the engine. (Completely, if it is reasonably practical.) The very first thing to look for is fuel leakage—wet spots on fuel lines and hoses and on carburetors, fuel pumps, fuel injection servos and at intake pipes and fuel injection spiders and nozzles. Next, check for oil leaks. You may be surprised. In one case, we knew we had a leak developing at the oil cooler of our Comanche, but we weren't prepared for the gusher that had covered the fuel pump on the accessory case. The culprit, as the accompanying illustration shows, was a chewed-up seal on the external oil lines to the oil cooler. All four of them needed to replaced. At the apparent leakage rate, the sump probably did not hold enough oil to last for much more than an hour's flight. There is no question that the oil leaks were a direct result of lack of activity by an otherwise very well-maintained airplane.

Oil leaks are common at pushrod tube seals, at external oil lines to oil coolers and oil filters, and from oil coolers and filter mounting plates. Dirty oil, incidentally, is easiest to spot, so this check is generally more effective before an oil change. Turbocharged aircraft have their own special sources of oil leaks with their myriad flexible lines. Look at any

In the case of one Comanche, this oil seal caused a sizable oil leak. Note the slight notch which permitted gross leakage.

Connections to the Comanche's oil cooler were undone in order to replace the oil seals.

The other end of the Comanche's oil lines. Older airplanes have aluminum rather than flex hose.

accessory mounting pads for leaks from their gaskets, and from the rocker box covers.

Once you are satisfied that oil leaks are under control, look for other fluid leaks. If you still have an assistant, have him or her operate the cockpit controls while you continue your investigating. Turn on the boost pump, if so equipped, and check for fuel leaks in the flexible line to the carburetor or fuel injector. Have your helper cycle the primer several times, so you can check for leaks at fittings (include any "T" fittings in the system, as well as those entering the cylinders). On fuel-injected engines, with the boost pump on, have

your helper run the mixture to rich, so you can check the fuel flow divider and lines for leaks. Check hydraulic systems in the same way, if you can run a hydraulic pump independent of the engine running.

If you have not already done so, have your helper cycle each of the engine controls throughout its range while you watch. For example, the mixture control should hit its carburetor stop while the mixture control knob is about an eighth of an inch from the cockpit panel stop. (The panel stop should not limit travel.) Heat and fresh-air vents should also be similarly adjusted, so that they reach full open or closed at the source, while remaining about an eighth of an inch from the panel stops. Check to see that each control is

The preventive maintenance of Lycoming engines calls for giving a blast of dry-lube spray to the ring gear and Bendix at the front (top photo) every week or two as well as periodically spraying the crossover slip joint (bottom photo) with penetrant to prevent seizing.

safetied, cottered, or otherwise secured against vibration shaking it free.

After all controls have been checked for travel, security and corrosion and abrading, inspect all flexible lines for flexibility; are they unfrayed and still limber? Modern lines are of Teflon and seem destined to last indefinitely.

Next, turn your attention to the engine and accessories. Check the condition and tension of generator or alternator belts. Are they uncracked, with about a half inch of displacement when you press on them between the pulleys? Are the screw clamps on the induction pipe hoses tight? Are the induction pipe hoses cracked, which can lead to induction leaks and rough running?

Check the condition of baffles and cooling air ram tubes for generators, alternators and magnetos. With a small mirror, look to see if all intake and exhaust studs have nuts on them. Do the nuts appear to be tight? Are there green or grey-brown exhaust stains around the exhaust stacks and their gaskets? It is common for such gaskets to blow every few hundred hours, which contributes mightily to cabin noise and results in a dramatic loss of efficiency and an incipient roughness.

Look over the exhaust system for cracks; for systems with crossover tubes, such as illustrated, squirt in a bit of WD-40, and you will avoid joint seizing, which can cause eventual cracking due to expansion at operating temperature. Hit the exposed end of a Bendix-type starter drive shaft with a squirt of silicon spray, and the Bendix will last twice as long as your buddy's.

In short, visually check everything. For the most part, airframes are well enough isolated from the vibration of powerplants that they don't shake apart. The same is not true of those items firewall-forward. The accompanying photographs show some examples of real as well as potential discrepancies. Don't be afraid to tighten the rocker box covers with a blade screwdriver, or to tighten any other hardware (except for critical items that were originally installed with torque wrenches), and don't hesitate to attack any landing gear grease zerks with a grease gun (with the appropriate grease).

Recowl the engine, inspect the propeller for leaks and nicks, then hit all exposed control hinges with a few drops of oil, as specified in the service manual. Polish the windshield and windows with Mirror Glaze (or equivalent), and you are just about ready to go flying. A nice touch is to dissolve a chunk of paraffin wax in white gas, and then paint the mixture onto the seat rails—especially on Cessnas. After the white gas evaporates, a film of wax remains, and the seats slide easily, almost as if they were designed that way.

If you can contain your enthusiasm for a few minutes extra, check the aircraft documents and logs. Make sure the Registration Certificate is current and on display. Pink slips expire after 120 days; and any superceded Registration Certificates are supposed to be returned to the FAA at OKC. At the least, they should be destroyed. Is the Airworthiness Certificate aboard? How about weight and balance documents and the Approved Flight Manual (required to be aboard when you fly)? Is the ELT battery expired? This gets most of us at some time. And what of the annual inspection? Most of us do just fine on the annual but don't understand that many AD notes are recurring and require compliance between annuals. One such is the Hartzell prop AD. Those props are good for five calendar years only—you could be illegal if the five years expires before annual time.

Enough of the wet-blanket stuff. Your airplane is now ready, and you know it is ready. You have virtually done a hundred-hour inspection, except for some of the engine's internal workings and a few things hidden behind inspection plates. You've earned a break, so go fly for a while, with confidence that the old flivver is truly ready for the opportunity.

RIGGING: WHAT EVERY PILOT SHOULD KNOW

One of the most mysterious and neglected facets of aircraft maintenance, it seems, is the proper rigging of airframes. In large part, this is the fault of pilots, who—through ignorance or innocence—are willing to tolerate airplanes that are out of rig. Unless a pilot complains about an aircraft flying "left wing low" (or whatever), the odds of a rigging problem being detected and corrected by an A&P during normal maintenance are tiny. There's a good reason for this. Mechanics can't tell that an airplane is out of rig by looking at it—it has to be flown.

Out-of-rig planes, besides being uncomfortable to fly, suffer significant reductions in efficiency (airspeed, rate of climb, et cetera); and, in certain instances, they can be downright unsafe to fly. Ailerons, either imbalanced or improperly tensioned, can flutter—and depart the aircraft. Among several horror stories vivid in our memory is the time one of us flew an Aero Commander twin one night and wrote it up as hopelessly out of rig. (The airplane flew sideways and rolled to the right quite nicely but showed little enthusiasm for left banks.) The plane had only recently been returned to service after sustaining substantial damage during a takeoff accident. This pilot had flown the aircraft soon after; but before maintenance could check into his writeup, the same Aero Commander—now being flown by another pilot—crashed fatally on its next flight, on an instrument approach.

Messages from the Inner Ear

Rigging an aircraft—or even making the initial diagnosis of an out-of-rig condition—is not for the heavyhanded. You have to "listen" (with your semi-circular canals) to what the airplane is telling you. As an example, one old Comanche—probably never rerigged in the 24 years since it left the Piper factory—was routinely (and annoyingly) left-wing-heavy until an hour and half of fuel was burned off from the left side. This was the case even though a fixed tab on the left aileron was bent to its maximum deflection (clear evidence that someone had tried, however crudely, to fix the problem). With a tensiometer and protractor, it was discovered that the right wing flap was drooped one degree lower than the left flap. During the course of rigging the airplane, the right flap pushrod was lengthened by unscrewing the rod end a single full turn—1/32 of an inch. Too much; that made a change of two degrees. The pushrod length was then *taken up* by a half turn and the desired setting was obtained. Also, the fixed tab on the aileron was neutralized. With all cable tensions and other control travels adjusted per the book, the airplane now flies true.

Of course, left-wing-low conditions are more common than right-wing-low, and it's possible to go through a long, painstaking, iterative rerigging procedure to correct a left-wing-low condition, only to find that when you put your partner or wife in the copilot's seat, the plane flies *starboard*-wing-low. So don't just correct for your weight on the pilot's side of the cabin. (Balance your own weight with fuel in the opposite wing so as to create *zero net lateral moment* before taking off.)

Bringing a Comanche (not this one) back into proper rig called for correcting some misguided steps by others as we diagnosed and fixed the real problem—asymmetric flap droop.

Wings without proper washout (negative twist toward the tip) can be tantalizing to fly, to put it lightly. Take the case of an old PA-11 (a full-cowled 95 hp Piper J-3). Oh, would that airplane climb! It would heft an awesome load and cruise significantly faster than any other PA-11 anyone had seen. For all that, though, its stall was incredibly nasty.

Sins of Commision and Omission

It was discovered that the wings were flat as boards. What had happened quickly became evident: The airplane had been used as a sprayer, and the last person to rebuild it had built up the wings without any washout (thereby upping the plane's performance and payload dramatically). But of course, without washout, a wing stalls all at once, at every point along the span—which is exactly what washout is supposed to prevent. It is not unusual, when you find a plane rigged in some novel fashion for it to have been in an accident of some kind. Planes have a way of not being returned to proper rig, once crunched.

Rigging an airplane—particularly one which has been damaged and repaired since leaving the factory—should begin with checking structural alignments and adjustments and aircraft symmetry. For very good reasons, these checks are done in a set sequence. The typical sequence is as follows:

1. Wing dihedral angle.
2. Wing incidence angle.
3. Engine alignment. (This may vary with horsepower within a given model series, for obvious reasons.)
4. Horizontal stabilizer incidence.
5. Horizontal stabilizer dihedral.
6. Vertical fin alignment.
7. Airframe symmetry.
8. Landing gear alignment.

The ability to make changes to any of the above items is largely dependent upon configuration: Wing dihedral and incidence angles are easy to adjust on most strut-braced wings (ditto horizontal stabilizer adjustments on Bellancas). At the opposite extreme, if you have differing wing incidence angles on your Mooney's single-piece wing—or if a symmetry check reveals that your Cessna 172's wing is displaced a half-inch at the tip—you have problems perhaps best solved by an attorney.

The finest of maintenance inspectors is a distrusting beast who

Among airplanes, rigging problems vary from configuration to configuration and from flight history to flight history, reflecting points of neglect or confusion that might otherwise escape detection.

assumes nothing. Yet most mechanics are without guile and, as a result, will often attempt to zero in on the crux of a problem without first assuring themselves that the necessary groundwork is perfect. (One of our editors learned this recently after he sold his Skylane and the new owner discovered—much to the surprise of everyone—that the plane's propeller had gone through six annuals without anyone bothering to crosscheck its actual serial number, as stamped on the hub, against the number shown in the aircraft logbooks.) As a matter of practice, mechanics seldom do symmetry and dimensional checks of wings, surfaces, etc., until after all the fixed tabs are all bent to the extreme, and the cables have all been tweaked, and a rigging problem still holds sway. Examples are a Super Cub that required left rudder on climbout, and a Cessna 170 (one of the most docile tail-draggers ever built) that kept trying to go off the runway to the right. The Super Cub's thrust line was offset too far to the right, and the 170's right gear was splayed to the right. Both aircraft had been rebuilt after substantial damage.

Notwithstanding the generous unassuming nature of mechanics, you—as an aircraft owner or operator—can legally *check* symmetry and airframe dimensions as carefully or as frequently as you like. Just grab your protractor and service manual, and have at it. If your aircraft has ever sustained major damage, go throught the whole regimen before tweaking any fixed tabs or rigging. Even if your aircraft was sold to you on the basis of 'NDH' (no damage history—which many aircraft salesmen consider a semantic problem), and if fixed tabs are bent significantly—or if control surfaces are out of trail position in normal cruise flight—you should suspect something wrong with the basic rigging.

Setting Up the Rig Check

It is important to dispel the notion that observing an aircraft's state of trim in flight is a subjective judgement call. A certain amount of piloting skill is called for, it's true; but there's nothing arbitrary about diagnosing an out-of-rig condition. By following a set procedure, it is possible to figure out whether or not the aircraft actually wants to fly sideways, or straight and level—even under the hood.

The very first step should be to take the aircraft out on a level spot on the ramp where you can run the engine. Level the aircraft about its roll axis, using the leveling points specified in the aircraft manual.

Proving out an aircraft's rigging means flying the plane precisely, in smooth air, and set up for its usual weight and balance.

(Many mechanics will simply lay a bubble level across the pilot's and copilot's seat tracks, then let air out of one or the other main tire to bring the aircraft level.) But again, be sure to correct for your own weight in the pilot's seat. Balance your own lateral moment with an equal moment of fuel in one wing. (It helps to have an assistant.)

After the aircraft has been levelled, adjust the turn coordinator or T&B so that the inclinometer ball is perfectly centered. (On most aircraft, this involves removing the Royalite false panel to get to the mounting screws, which ride in elongated adjustment slots. Then, too, many aircraft have shock-mounted gyro panels—in which case, it should be noted that sagging shock mounts can have an effect on the ball's position.)

Next, chock the wheels and take all appropriate precautions about whirling propellers. Have your assistant watch for hazards, as you will be distracted in the following steps. Start your engine and let the artificial horizon come up to speed. If the horizon bar is not level about the roll axis, adjust it as you did the turn coordinator. (It is also set in elongated adjustment slots.) Then shut down the engine and check to see that the cowl flaps retract uniformly, that both wing flaps appear to fully retract, and that any landing gear doors seem to be reasonably tightly mounted with no undue slack in pushrods or links.

Next, using a straightedge, bring any movable aileron or rudder tabs into trail (don't trust trim tab indicators for this—although you should note their position). Fill the fuel tanks completely, empty out the baggage bay and/or wing lockers, and install a similarly overweight person in the right front seat (or fly solo if you prefer the aircraft to be rigged for mainly solo flights). Then take off and see how she flies. (It goes without saying that this flight should be conducted in smooth air.)

Accelerate to your normal cruise speed and establish level flight. Use elevator trim as needed, but don't touch the aileron or rudder trim just yet. With your feet off the ruder pedals, roll the wings level, referring to your freshly adjusted artificial horizon. Is one wing heavy? Is the ball on the turn coordinator askew? Do not touch the aileron trim; instead, apply rudder pressure to press the inclinometer ball back into its cage. Trim the rudder tab until this pressure is relieved, then note and record the new rudder trim setting. Chances are, once the ball is centered, any wing-heaviness will go away. If not, adjust the aileron trim until the pressure is relieved, and again note the setting. Few people realize that this is the proper sequence for trimming an aircraft for level flight. Use this procedure for all your flights.

For aircraft without movable rudder and aileron tabs, follow the same steps, pressing the ball to the center with the wings held level and writing down the nature and magnitude of control forces required to hold the plane in level flight.

Obviously, if constant control pressure is required—or if fixed tabs must be bent out of their trail positions—you are giving away airspeed, and a further check of rigging will pay definite dividends in performance.

Symmetry

Basic symmetry and dimensional checks can be done without specialized tools. For this you'll need only a three- or four-foot carpenter's level, 50-foot tape measure, paint stirring stick, a 12-inch adjustable square, a chalk line, some tape, and some short stacks of washers or coins.

The design of your aircraft has much significance when we discuss dimensional checks. While Piper was still building airframes of steel tubes that twanged into odd contortions after release from the jigs, Beech was building the first of its Bonanzas with the closest of tolerances, on Class A tooling. A turn here on a threaded strut fork, and a turn there on the flying wires, and all the ragbag Pipers could be made to fly about the same. Such a capacity for adjustment was neither built in nor necessary for aircraft like the Bonanza (barring damage in the field). The all-metal Mooney, with its wing all of a piece, carries the lack of adjustment even further. Whatever dihedral, incidence, and washout that wing has was built into it on Day One at the factory.

So although we'll discuss each of the symmetry and dimensional checks in some detail, bear in mind that it's possible not all of them will be applicable to your plane. (Consult your service manual for a more definitive methodology.)

Try to conduct all of the following checks on level ground, with the plane level about the roll axis (and the pitch axis too, if possible); and pick a windless day, if you are outside, to preclude errors due to wind shifting or strut settling.

Dihedral Check

The aircraft must be leveled about its roll axis. Like any of the other checks, this is most easily accomplished with a propeller protractor (such as is used for magneto timing); however, it can also be done using the simple tools described above. With bits of tape, mark off spots on each wing that are identical distances from skin laps or

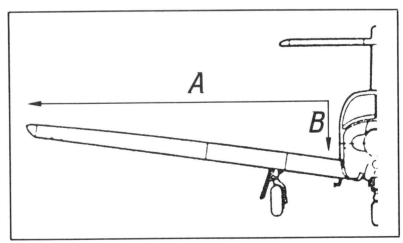

In the dihedral check, the ratio of A to B (i.e., the tangent of the dihedral angle) should be the same for each wing.

other readily identifiable points of wing construction symmetry. Spots on the spar are most appropriate. With the carpenter's level parallel to or on top of the spar, stack washers or coins under the lower end of the level until its bubble is centered, then measure the included angle with the dimestore protractor. Do the same for the opposite wing. The trig-happy reader will be quick to realize that, strictly speaking, a protractor isn't necessary here, since the included angle (which is the same as your dihedral angle) can be figured from the ratio of A to B, where A is the coin-stack height and B is the length of the level. If you calculate A over B, and look up that number in a table of tangents (or simply hit the inverse-tan button on your pocket calculator), you can find the angle that it represents. Obviously, A/B for the left wing should equal A/B for the right wing.

It's possible that the dihedral angle for both wings is equal, but not as specified in the service manual. (Severe air gusts have been known to change dihedral angles.) If the actual dihedral angle is not of interest to you, but you merely want to check symmetry, then compare coin-stack heights (dimension A above). If there is no adjustment for dihedral on your plane (check the manual), any discrepancy in wing heights should mean a search for hidden damage due to hard landing or gust loads, since aircraft manufacturers rarely miss on dihedral.

Wing Incidence

Unfortunately, the days of flat-bottomed airfoils are gone forever, and wing incidence (and washout) checks are no longer as simple as they once were. Ideally, service manuals should describe a method of making incidence boards, giving specific points along the wing where the boards could be used to actually measure the angle of incidence. Few manuals give such procedures, as it turns out. But we can do a simple spot check of symmetry (which is primarily what we're concerned with here anyway) as follows.

Using tape or C-clamps, join a straightedge to one end of your carpenter's level, and—with the aircraft leveled (on jacks, if need be)—lay the whole affair chordwise (parallel to the slipstream) on top of the wing, at a specific wing station, with the straightedge portion sticking forward. Next, with the level touching the wing skin (avoid any "canning") and the bubble centered, use the adjustable square to obtain dimensions on the level. Record the dimensions.

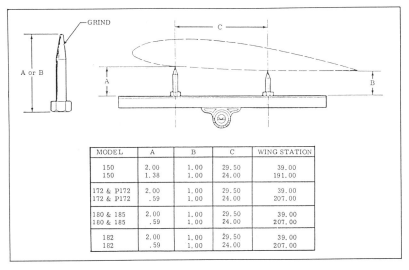

MODEL	A	B	C	WING STATION
150	2.00	1.00	29.50	39.00
150	1.38	1.00	24.00	191.00
172 & P172	2.00	1.00	29.50	39.00
172 & P172	.59	1.00	24.00	207.00
180 & 185	2.00	1.00	29.50	39.00
180 & 185	.59	1.00	24.00	207.00
182	2.00	1.00	29.50	39.00
182	.59	1.00	24.00	207.00

The Cessna procedure for checking wing twist (washout) involves placing a bubble level underneath the wing and gauging the twist via ground-off bolts of specific length.

Keep everything parallel to the slipstream and make sure your alignment with the apparatus is identical as you move from wing to wing. Both wings should measure the same, at stations near the root; and very nearly the same at the tip (as long as the washout for each wing is the same). If the dimensions are off more than a few percent—and your aircraft drops off on one wing in the stall—you may have reason to investigate further.

A variation of the above procedure is called out in the Cessna service manuals. Cessna has the observer place the level *under* each wing, then measure the daylight remaining between wing and level at specific points using bolts that have been ground to specific lengths (see accompanying diagram). Note that in most Cessnas, all washout (twist) occurs outboard of the struts.

Not all airplanes are symmetric: The Bonanza service manual suggests rigging the wings so that the right wing is adjusted with its trailing edge at the highest adjustment point, and the left wing trailing edge set down 1/16th-inch from the highest adjustment point. (The total available adjustment for each wing is about 1/8th-inch.)

Wing root adjustments are, incidentally, usually made by turning small bushing-like eccentrics at the rear spar attach points. Outboard differences in incidence—in strutted wings—are adjusted by lengthening or shortening the rear strut fork. On single-strut and strutless metal wings, manufacturing tolerances are pretty good concerning wing twist, so again, if there is an inconsistency, assume that some damage was repaired with a faulty jig—or no jig.

Airframe Symmetry

If your plane was crashed in the Amazon jungle, then repaired poorly, you'll be able to tell it by this check. Put away the level and protractor; whip out the tape measure. Measure from each wing tip to a spot near the base of the vertical fin, or the rudder post. (Do not measure to the front of the fin, as most vertical stabilizers are offset slightly to compensate for slipstream effects, or what many pilots mistakenly refer to as "torque.") This is a check for lateral displacement of a wing, a classic indication of damage.

This same sort of check can (and should) be done for the tail, to check for displacement of, say, the horizontal stabilizer. Just take similar measurements from the tips of the horizontal stab to definable, identical points on the forward fuselage (such as wing spar fittings or strut attach points). Other relationships on your airframe may present themselves, such as dimensions from the rudder post to fixed points on the landing gear legs. (This may tell you something about your gear legs!) Bonanza owners beware: If you measure the distance from any point on the left side of the plane to the nose gear casing, and any right-side point to the nose gear, you'll get two unequal numbers. The nose gear is not on the centerline.

Again, the primary purpose of these checks is to assure that the airframe has no hidden damage (or at least that such damage has been repaired properly).

Engine Alignment

This check can be considered optional, if the airplane is 'NDH' (no damage history). Many aircraft have displaced thrustlines, normally. The reason for this is to minimize rudder force needed in climb; assist in stall recovery; and/or to compensate for torque, P-effects, and slipsteam curvature around the fuselage and tail. With the aircraft leveled in roll *and* pitch (on jacks), the degree of down thrustline can be measured by placing a level across the tops of the cylinders, parallel to the crankshaft. What you're really measuring here, on older aircraft, is the droop due to engine mount deterioration. Replacing those old motor mounts can often pay surprising dividends not only in added thrust, but in reduced drag: any engine-to-cowl baffling will draw up and seal better. You get better cooling, less drag, lowered vibration, less noise, *and* a more consistent thrust vector.

But how about measuring the right/left thrustline displacement? (It had better be to the right, if it's an American-built plane.) Start by dropping a plumb bob line from the center of the rudder post to the ground, marking the spot with a bit of chalk, then doing the same at identical points near each wingtip. From each of the marks below the wingtips, swing arcs of identical length (20 or 30 feet) forward, and mark the point where these two arcs cross. Run a chalkline between the point you just made, and the point under the rudder post, snap the chalkline, and you will have found the centerline of the aircraft (shifted to the ground, of course).

If you now drop a plumb line from the tip of the spinner, it should be clear exactly how much your thrustline is displaced from the center. To get the precise *angle*, however, you'll need to drop plumbs from the prop tips, mark the spots, and measure the angle by which the prop plane is shifted from the direction of flight. Check your results against the specs given in your service manual. Usually, the thrustline is offset no more than two or three degrees. If it's more than this (i.e., you need left rudder in a climb), check for engine-mount or firewall damage.

Landing Gear Alignment

Unusual tire wear is often a tipoff to poor landing gear alignment. Another indication is when a normally docile aircraft behaves squirrelly on the ground. There's more than just parallel alignment to consider, however. Proper alignment means correct toe-in and camber, too. (Toe-in is the same as pigeon-toedness, looking from above the aircraft; camber is seen from a front-on perspective and is "positive" when the tops of the main gear tires are further apart than the bottoms, and "negative" when the bottoms are splayed out relative to the tops.)

For the most part, manufacturers recommend zero toe-in and zero camber *at maximum gross weight,* and some means of shimming the gear is normally provided. With oleo-strutted Pipers and Beeches, camber is not adustable, although toe-in and parallel alignment can be set by adding or subtracting washers from the torque knees on the oleo scissors. With Wittman-style (spring steel) gear, a la Cessna and Citabria, shims are used at the wheel/axle to change camber and toe-in. (Shims are also used at the fuselage to adjust gear height.) Considerable positive camber may be normal at reduced ramp weights.

The alignment technique preferred by Cessna is to hold a long straightedge across and between both main gear tires, at wheel hub height, while the wheel to be checked is resting on a sandwich of two aluminum plates with wheel grease between the plates. (The greased plates eliminate tire friction and allow the gear to shift freely with the Wittman springs in a relieved state.) Then, using a carpenter's square held against the straightedge, you can measure toe-in at the edges of the wheels. Total toe-in (both wheels added together) should not exceed .12-inch for Cessna taildraggers; .06-inch for trike types. This is with cabin and fuel tanks empty. (A protractor is used to measure camber; lay the protractor vertically on the wheel diameter. Camber under these conditions should be about 5 degrees positive. At gross weight, this will become zero degrees.)

The above technique can be used (sans grease pads) for oleo-strutted aircraft, and in fact is called out as such in the Piper Cherokee service manual. The only difference is, you'll need a much longer straightedge (i.e., a 12-foot piece of angle iron) to reach between the tires. Remember that a toe-in on one wheel and a toe-*out* of the other wheel may add up to zero net toe-in, but gives you a sideways-taxiing aircraft—very hard on tires during landing. (For further details about checking wheel alignment, see Chapter 6.)

To level your airplane for certain airframe symmetry and rigging checks, you may have to raise it on jacks. That may give you pause, but the operation need not be difficult or dangerous if you know what you are doing.

Just as it is important to check and correct how your plane is rigged, it is incumbent upon you to confirm and, if necessary, look into elements of the control system, particularly the pulleys and cables. We have discussed this area generally with respect to the post-annual check, but this examination may be called for at any time. Unfortunately, it is too much neglected.

EXAMINING PULLEYS AND CABLES

When was the last time your control-system pulleys were inspected? Perhaps you've come to the conclusion that since this is what annual inspections are for, pulleys aren't something a pilot should spend time worrying about. Or maybe your plane is so new, you figure pulley problems are out of the question. In either case, you'd be wrong.

We have seen airplanes come out of annual inspection with frozen pulleys (more than once); and in the case of new airplanes undergoing their first 100-hour, the incidence of cable and pulley problems (misrouting, chafing, etc) is in our opinion nothing short of shocking. (FAA records show some 330 reports of cable/pulley problems in less-than-200-hour-old aircraft in the past five years.) The standard procedure now at many shops seems to be to inspect only easily visible pulleys (and then only in the static condition) for obvious damage and/or misrouting of cables. *Thorough* inspection of pulleys and cables seems to be a forgotten art (to say nothing of control-system troubleshooting on the basis of pulley wear patterns).

Sticking Points

Stuck pulleys are a fairly common problem, especially in older aircraft. What happens is, the grease inside the pulley's bearings begins to cake and harden over time—a process that might take a lot longer to begin in a bearing that's subject to *continual rotation*, but in a pulley (where the motion is back and forth, over a short arc only) occurs

Pulleys are often so deeply buried, they may be poorly examined or escape inspection entirely over several months.

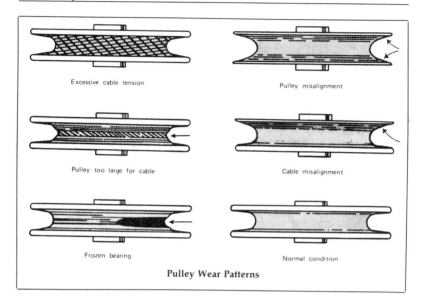

Excessive cable tension

Pulley misalignment

Pulley too large for cable

Cable misalignment

Frozen bearing

Normal condition

Pulley Wear Patterns

quickly. Before the pulley actually freezes solid, its "working arc" diminishes. It may only rotate through 10 or 20 degrees of arc.) Finally, at some point, the pulley sticks (zero rotation). Then—since the cable has only one bare spot to rub against—asymmetric wear of the groove begins. And as the cable sinks lower and lower into the groove, control system tension degrades. Not by much, at first—but factor in all the *other* pulleys that might be wearing and/or sticking at the same time throughout the airframe, and you can see how 10 or 20 pounds of cable tension can mysteriously be lost in a year's time. (Of course, cable tension is also temperature-dependent—but that's another story.)

Two things you can do yourself: First, unstick any frozen pulleys you find by giving them a well-directed blast of LPS-2, Mouse Milk or WD-40. (Note that you can't detect frozen pulleys by simply look-ing at them. *Grab the pulley and try to rotate it, or have someone in the cockpit move the control system as you observe pulley operation.*) Work the unstuck pulley back and forth by hand until you are satisfied it is free. *Do not* attempt to free a difficult pulley by backing off on the re-tainer nut. If extra lube won't free it up, call in an A&P at once.

Secondly: *Rotate* the pulley to a new wear spot. Many pilots—and mechanics, it seems—have forgotten (or didn't know) that because most pulleys turn through an arc of less than 360 degrees, it is easy for pulleys to become worn preferentially in one spot during normal operation. The cure for this, of course, is to hand-rotate the pulley 180 degrees at each inspection (so as to "even up" the wear on both sides of the pulley). Ask your mechanic whether he did this at your last annual. You may be surprised at his response.

A third thing you can do—aided perhaps by an inspection mirror—is examine your pulleys for abnormal wear (see accompanying drawings). Pulley and cable misalignment are easily spotted, if you know what to look for. Access may be a problem, though.

While you're at it, give the control cables a good visual once-over, looking especially for fraying, chafing, misrouting, and slack tension. (You don't need a $100 tensiometer to detect dangerously slack cables.) Be sure cables are not wrapped together, or routed over (instead of under) cable guards. In general, cables should touch nothing metallic, including each other. (Another good rule of thumb: Unseemly squeaks or screeches of any kind while controls are in motion indicates items needing attention.)

Do not overlubricate cables or pulleys. Cables are meant to run dry, and sealed bearings need no periodic relubrication, unless indicated by your service manual. (You do have a service manual, don't you?) Use only a light, spray type lube, and then only as needed.

Properly maintained, ordinary AN220 control pulleys have been known to function flawlessly for 20 years or more—not bad, by aircraft (or any other) standards. Considering the inattention most pulleys receive at the hands of shops and owners, it's a wonder our AN220s last as long as they do. Yours, of course, will now last longer.

Gaining Greater Access

Checking out pulleys—or turnbuckles or wire bundles—can be an ordeal of lying on one's back in the dark and working by the Braille method simply because the access holes are in the wrong place. It is legal for an owner to add access holes and to make small patches and other reinforcements. (The patches must not change the contour in a way that interferes with proper airflow.) How valuable this capability can be is indicated by the fact that Cessna permits operators to add up to five new access holes in each wing of a Skyhawk, Skylane, or 150. Even the factory realizes that some things can't be reached through normal access holes.

It is strongly recommended that you obtain the supervision of an A&P

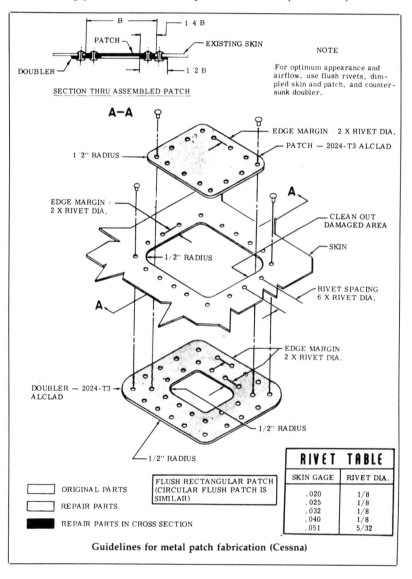

Guidelines for metal patch fabrication (Cessna)

NOTE

For optimum appearance and airflow, use flush rivets, dimpled skin and patch, and countersunk doubler.

SECTION THRU ASSEMBLED PATCH

A–A

RIVET TABLE	
SKIN GAGE	RIVET DIA.
.020	1/8
.025	1/8
.032	1/8
.040	1/8
.051	5/32

ORIGINAL PARTS

REPAIR PARTS

REPAIR PARTS IN CROSS SECTION

FLUSH RECTANGULAR PATCH
(CIRCULAR FLUSH PATCH IS SIMILAR)

mechanic prior to attempting the kinds of work described here.

The basic procedure for making an access hole is quite simple: After establishing the exact location for your access plate, scribe centerlines. Next, determine the position of your doubler with relation to the access hole and center it over the centerlines. Tip: Rather than fabricate the doubler yourself, you can buy the part pre-made (P/N S-1443-1) from your local Cessna dealer. (The Cessna doubler comes with Tinnerman nuts already installed and rivet holes pre-drilled.)

With the doubler centered over the centerlines, mark the rivet hole locations and drill .098 (No. 40) holes as shown at right. Then cut out a standard-size (5.062-in.) access hole (buy or borrow a sheet-metal circle-cutter), insert the doubler through the hole (flex it), and rivet the doubler in place.

All that remains is to fabricate or buy a standard inspection cover (Cessna P/N S-225-4F), grab a handful of screws (P/N S-1022Z-8-6), and attach the cover to the airframe. You can paint the inspection cover at your leisure.

Cessna's Service Department offers the following additional guidelines when installing access holes in wings:

1. Locate new access holes near the center of a bay (spanwise) whenever possible.

2. When working forward of the front spar, locate new access holes as close to the front spar as possible.

3. When working aft of the front spar, locate new inspection covers between the first and second stringers aft of the spar (consult appropriate service manual). Orient the doubler so that the two straight edges are closest to the stringers.

4. It is preferable to stagger access holes forward and aft of the front spar, in alternate bays, whenever possible.

5. Do not add access holes in the same bay where one is already located. Work through landing light installations where possible, instead of adding access holes. Also, do not add inspection covers to the outbyard end of either wing, when you can remove the wingtip for access.

6. If more than five new access holes are needed in either wing, contact the Cessna Service Department.

Skin cracks, punctures, and pinholes can be repaired by riveting a circular metal patch over a hole cut to the above dimensions—but why make a permanent skin patch when you can just as easily have an inspection cover (especially a cover that looks like it was installed by the factory)?

Considering the time and aggravation that a properly located access cover can save you, the do-it-yourself access hole may be one of the best bargains of all time.

CONTROL-CABLE RIGGING

Most pilots aren't accustomed to thinking of control-cable rigging as a seasonal type of maintenance, but it is. Cold weather makes cable tensions go down dramatically, because the coefficient of thermal expansion of an aluminum airframe differs significantly from that of steel control cables. Aluminum expands twice as much. As a result, control cables that are drum-tight in July can be as slack as linguini in January.

The chances are that your aileron cables currently are slack to the point of inviting flutter at high altitude or high airspeed and that all that is saving you is proper mass balance. Perhaps. How can you know unless you check it out?

As far as we know, only Beech, among the small-aircraft manufacturers, goes to the trouble of providing detailed service-manual

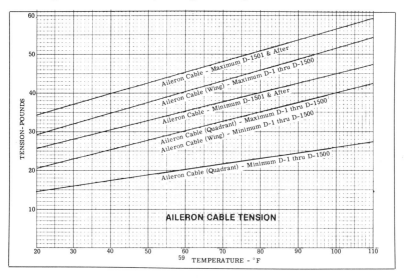

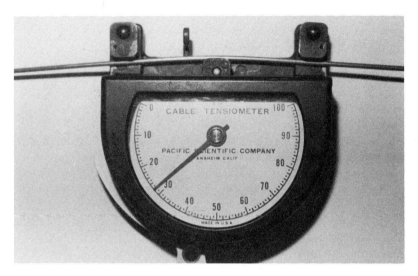

Fine-quality tensiometers like the one shown here can cost hundreds of dollars. Less expensive versions are available through sources in Trade-A-Plane. Fortunately, you do not need an extremely accurate tool for most tension checks, nor is a mechanic's signoff needed to check cable tensions yourself, as long as the cables are not altered in any way.

specs that quantify seasonal changes. Even with fairly short runs of cables (in a Bonanza), the effect can be dramatic. For example, the accompanying graph shows minimum and maximum aileron cable tensions for Beech 35-series airplanes, plotted against temperature. At 20 degrees Fahrenheit, the maximum aileron cable tension for Bonanza S/Ns D-1501 and after is 34 pounds; at 110 F, the max allowable tension zooms to almost 60 pounds. Adjusting tension requires that the mechanic set tension somewhere between the minimum and maximum for a given temperature; the properties of the metals will then keep cable tension between the limits throughout the normally encountered temperature range. Implicit in the procedure is the caveat that cables set at 50 or 60 pounds in a cold hangar, on a cold day (when tension should be closer to 30 pounds) could become so taut on a trip south—into warmer weather—that they might fail the pulley brackets or cable attach points.

If a tension-vs.-OAT chart is not given in your service manual, assume (unless specified otherwise) that all cables are to be tensioned in a 59-degree F hangar.

Tools & Preparation

There is certainly nothing illegal about your *checking* control-cable tensions, control surface travel, etc. Making actual rigging adjustments yourself is not preventive maintenance, though, so to carry out some of the steps described here you'll need a mechanic's supervision and sign-off if you want to remain legal. It's essential, in any careful check of rigging, to have conducted careful dimensional and symmetry checks prior to attacking systems with protractor and tensiometer in hand. Only *after* you are positive that such variables as wing incidence and dihedral meet factory specs can you do a proper job of rigging.

With the airframe dimensional and symmetry checks completed as described earlier in this chapter, the control surfaces themselves can come under scrutiny—not only for cable tensions, but for overall

Tensiometers are supplied with various sizes of riser blocks to be used with various cable thicknesses. Here, the No. 2 risers are used with 5/32 cable (actually, welding rod)..

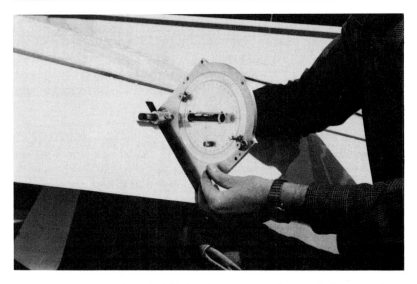

Using a protractor with a bubble level to measure the travel of a control surface, in this case, the left flap of a Comanche.

throw (arc of travel), limit stops, and neutral positions. Because each aircraft type is subject to many variables in the exact procedures to be followed, our recommendations will at times necessarily be general; so (as usual) before doing anything to *your* airplane, be sure to consult the appropriate service manual.

The tool list is short but impressively expensive if you want to get the job done right:

1. Propeller protractor. (Best borrowed, as the retail price is now well over $400.) A quick-and-dirty substitute may be improvised with a student-quality protractor and small level, or with simple tools available at the hardware store.

2. Cable tensiometer. (Again, this can be expensive. For instance, the tensiometer illustrated in this chapter costs in the hundreds. Tool advertisers in *Trade-a-Plane*, however, list inexpensive tensiometers for less than $100. These may not be as precise as the highest-priced models, but the tension limits for most aircraft allow enough latitude to make the use of a moderately priced tension tool acceptable.) See below for operating instructions.

3. Carpenter's level.

4. Straightedge.

Before and during any cable-tension checks, it is important to see that the pulleys are turning freely, properly lubed, and not worn, that the cables are not frayed, and that the rod ends on the pushrods are clean and free. (Refer to the examination and corrective procedures in the preceding section.)

How to Use Protractors and Tensiometers

The professional grade tensiometer is said to be 98-percent accurate when properly maintained. To use the usual type, as illustrated in the accompanying photographs, it is first necessary to determine the control cable diameter, and refer to the tensiometer calibration chart which comes with the tensiometer to ascertain which riser should be installed. In the case of the illustration, the No. 2 riser (of a set of three risers) was recommended for the cable diameter in question. (For purposes of illustration, a piece of welding rod was used, in lieu of standing on our ears with a camera in the hell-hole of an airplane.)

With the trigger lever at the bottom of the gauge swung out to its open position, the riser is retracted, then the cable is placed between the two ears at the top, known as anvils. Then the trigger is closed, which extends the riser, and a reading may be taken. The small lever at the top of the instrument is a pointer lock, which is used when access for viewing is limited. With it, the instrument can be draped over a hidden cable, the trigger can be closed and then released, and the pointer reading will be held for reading.

In the illustrated tension check, the eighth-inch welding rod, presumed to be 5/32 cable, shows a raw reading of about 28. That dial reading is converted to tension by referring to the appropriate chart and interpolating. In this case, we would have a tension of 65 pounds—just right for that cable size if I had checked it at 25 degrees Fahrenheit! In practice, the desired tension is obtained from the aircraft manufacturer's rigging information, and that number is converted back to a desired tensiometer reading.

The universal propeller protractor, in the manner in which we use it for checking control travels, gives us relative checks, as it doesn't have a locking pin to pin the vernier ring of disk degree scale either parallel to or at right angles to the three straight edges of the protractor frame. For the most part, such a function isn't necessary. For ex-

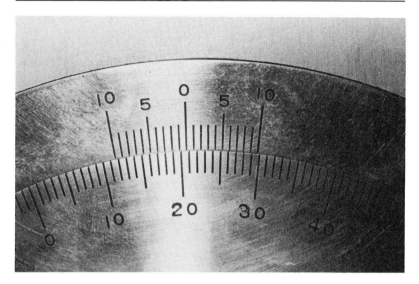

The vernier scale on a prop protractor is read in degrees and tenths. Here, the reading is 20.7 degrees—not 27 degrees.

ample, to obtain neutral on our stabilator, we need to level the aircraft and then use a carpenter's level and rigging boards to do the job properly. (How nice if all manuals were to give us a dimensional check to verify the stabilator's neutral position at its leading edge.)

For absolute accuracy in using the prop protractor, the airplane should be level about its roll axis before checking control surface rigging. Leveling about the pitch axis is unnecessary, because the protractor's measurements are relative, not absolute. Just be careful not to climb up on a wingwalk or do anything else that will change the nose attitude during the rigging checks.

Here's how it works: let's say you have the flaps rigged, and want to check the ailerons for proper travel. Often, the aircraft service manual will tell us to align the aileron and flap trailing edges. In that case, *make sure that the flaps have already been rigged properly*. Then, with the aileron temporarily clamped in place to the flap's trailing edge, follow this sequence:

1. With the disk degree scale and ring vernier scale locked on zero and the control surface in neutral, place the protractor on the control

surface and then turn the ring adjuster until the center spirit level bubble is centered.

2. Tighten the ring-to-frame lock thumbscrew.

3. Unclamp the aileron and move it up or down to one or the other of its limit stops.

4. Unlock the disk degree scale from the ring vernier scale.

5. Turn the disk adjuster to again center the bubble in the center spirit level. Tighten the lock screw.

6. Read the surface travel in degrees on the disk and tenths of a degree on the vernier scale. The illustration shows a control deflection of 20.7 degrees.

If you want to get fancy, the other spirit bubble can be turned out perpendicular to the protractor face, and the protractor can be held level while taking readings. Such accuracy is hardly necessary if you are reasonably careful about holding the protractor perpendicular to the control surface skin.

For those who cannot borrow a propeller protractor, and who consider the expense of buying one to be extra-ordinary, a good hardware store offers two simple alternatives:

1. Buy a small carpenter's variable angle try-square. Use it in conjunction with any sort of bubble level such as the small one built into 12-inch adjustable squares. Adjust it as shown in the accompanying illustration, until the bubble is level. Then read the included angle with a child's school protractor. This should be accurate within half a degree, if you are careful. That is well within the tolerances for control throws spelled out in your service manual.

2. Buy a small machinist's protractor, and use it with the same sort of bubble level. This works almost as nicely as the more expensive prop protractor yet only costs two percent as much.

Cable Tension Adjustment

Mechanics have complained that setting Cessna control cable tensions to factory specs results in the controls' being stiff and hard to move when the aircraft is at rest. We have noticed a similar situation with a Comanche, but it didn't have a noticeable effect on actually flying the aircraft. Our inclination is to abide by the factory specs even though the cable tension may seem excessive from the cockpit; for whatever friction is induced is really only a small fraction of flight control loading. As such, it isn't noticeable, and the control feel is much more positive throughout a wider range of conditions, approaching the feel of pushrod-actuated controls. (What those mechanics don't realize, perhaps, is that angular displacement of the yoke and control surfaces is relatively small when the craft is airborne; thus, angular friction doesn't come into play.)

Cable tension is adjusted by means of turnbuckles on all contemporary aircraft with cable-actuated controls. (Mooney owners can skip most of this.) The turnbuckles are generally of brass, although both cadmium-plated steel and anodized aluminum alloy are also available. Earlier aircraft turnbuckles used lockwire for safetying, but newer aircraft use clip-locking turnbuckles, in which two locking clips—with the turnbuckle barrel and terminals slotted lengthwise to accommodate the locking clips—are employed. After the cable tensions are adjusted, the slots in the barrels and the slots in the terminals are aligned and the clips are inserted.

Turnbuckles work the way they do (to take up slack or let it out) because one end of the barrel is left-hand threaded, while the other end is right-hand threaded; rotating the turnbuckle barrel takes up the length in both ends, increasing the cable tension. It should be evident why safetying or locking clips are necessary—vibration could easily allow the barrel components to rotate and cause the cables to separate.

Adjusting the aileron control cable tension offers some opportunity to work out some rigging or aileron droop problems. (Note that checking and adjusting cable tension is or should be considered a preliminary step to adjustments involving control travel.) Designs vary, of course. But with the control yoke(s) secured and unmoving, tightening of any one turnbuckle will normally result in deflection of at least one of the ailerons, along with concurrent displacement of bellcranks and pushrods. In the Comanche's case, it is important to use the aileron bellcrank template to assure that the bellcranks are not improperly displaced as tension is increased (or, as is often the case, decreased). Cable tension is set with the tensiometer, while taking the above caveat into consideration. On many aircraft, it is necessary to assure that the bicycle chain that is draped over the aileron drive sprockets is centered, since if one were to start rigging at the ailerons and work backwards to the control yoke, this chain could be dangerously shifted.

Remember that cable-actuated ailerons always have some type of interconnect; and the interconnect cable turnbuckle may be hard to find.

As you might guess, there is a lot of trial and error and repeated

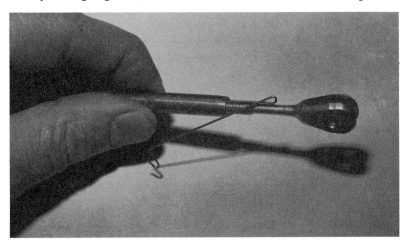

Most late-model airplanes use clippable MS21251-type turnbuckles with a grooved barrel and shaft to accept the clip.

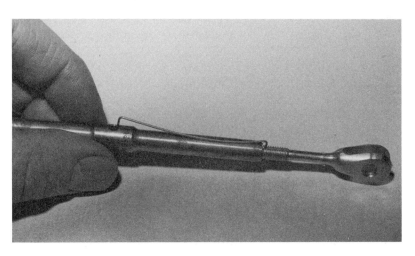

Here, the safety clip has been installed in the turnbuckle to prevent rotation of the barrel. The clip eliminates the need for elaborate safety-wiring.

recheckings of tensions and control surface and bellcrank positions in getting the ailerons—or any other closed system of cables—properly rigged. If the system is designed for the use of rigging pins, a lot of chasing back and forth is unnecessary—the pins are put in place at the yoke and at the bellcranks, and then the final tensions of each of the cables is merely set to spec. Done properly, the rigging pins should not even be finger-tight when they are removed.

After the tensions are set on the aileron cables, with the yokes in neutral and the bellcranks where they belong, bellcrank-to-aileron pushrods are set, adjusting the ailerons into proper trail position. Then it is only a simple matter of checking the control surface travel or throw with the prop protractor or the other suggested implements. There is no reason for the aileron throws to be be wrong if everything else (see above; see below) has been done properly, with the possible exception of the control limit stops being set wrong.

Limit Stops

You may not have known it, but each aileron, elevator, rudder, or stabilator is—by regulation—designed to have both primary and secondary control limit stops. The primary stops are at or near the control surface, sometimes where you can see them (as with Cessna rudder stops), but most frequently they are located at the control horn or bellcrank.

The secondary stops are located at the other end of the cable or pushrod runs, somewhere close to the control yoke or rudder pedals. They are to be set so that the primary control stops actually limit the surface travel. Then, if excessive force is exerted on the cockpit controls, whatever slack or give in the system exists will be taken up and the secondary control stop limits will be run into.

Whatever you do, don't make the (common) mistake of moving the control surfaces externally when checking the control stops, or when checking control travels with a protractor (see below). In either case, the control should be displaced by going to the maximum yoke displacement, then checking the deflection with the protractor, or checking to see that the deflection was great enough to meet the control limit stops. As you may imagine, once tension is set and the control deflection is checked, the limit stops are set to the manufacturer's control throws, usually to a one- or two-degree tolerance. The point to remember is that if the primary limit stop requires resetting, it will almost always be necessary to readjust the secondary stops.

Surface Travel: Flaps

A good place to start when checking surface travels is with the flaps, because the techniques used are common to those used for rigging the other controls as well (although neutralizing the cockpit controls is not necessary). A typical method is to use either a propeller protractor or—more commonly—a straightedge to assure that the flaps are in trail position when they are retracted. The straightedge is merely held perpendicular to the wing spar on the bottom of the wing, somewhere along the span of the flap. Once you are certain that the straightedge is not resting on any rivets or bulges, it is desirable that it be flush with the bottom of the airfoil and with the flap's leading and trailing edges.

If the flap is slightly drooped (particularly with cable-actuated flaps), it is worth the effort to push up lightly at its trailing edge to see if it is completely against its upper limit stop. Certain uplock mechanisms can be worn, and the cable tension can be too loose. In such cases—as with ailerons—a slight droop due to cable play and gravity can be tolerated, as aerodynamic loads will cause the flaps to fly into trail (or up-against-the-stop position). Some aircraft have ailerons that are rigged with droop purposely, for this very reason, although it would normally be counterproductive to rig either flaps *or* ailerons with droop deliberately. More typically, when flaps are drooping, all that's needed (especially with the old Johnson-bar-on-the-floor manual types) is for the cable slack to be taken up, in accordance with the service manual. If the flap cable tension isn't specified, bringing them up to 15-20 lbs. tension should be about right.

When your aircraft is equipped with hydraulic flaps (Aero Commanders, various Piper products), or electric flaps (Cessna and Beech products), make certain that they are fully retracted by using the switches and standby hydraulic pumps, as equipped and necessary. Any deviation from trail position will require a check of limit stops and limit switches, and possibly of pushrod lengths.

In any case, what's most important here is to assure that *both* flaps are rigged the same way—with identical droop or trail. Any difference is normally adjusted by shortening or lengthening the respective pushrod from the bellcrank to the flap pushrod bracket. Go easy on this: we found that the geometry is such that shortening the pushrod length by 1/32-inch (one turn on one of the rod ends) made a two-degree change on a flap's rigging, on our Comanche. Of course, wing-heaviness can be reduced by drooping the affected wing's flap. Normally, however, most people resort to bending a fixed tab—or, in the case of Mooneys, bending down the entire trailing edge of an aileron (within narrow limits; see your manual).

Those willing to experiment can find significant short-field takeoff performance gains by rigging the flaps and ailerons down a couple of degrees—or you can enjoy corresponding increases in cruising speeds and takeoff rolls by rigging both the flaps and the ailerons up a bit (with some sacrifice in control authority). Realize, of course, that you will become a test-pilot each time you fly, and the aircraft would not be—from a strict interpretation of Part 43—airworthy.

After you have made certain the flaps are in trail, and you have adjusted cable tensions, pushrod length, and limit stops until the flap rigging is symmetrical, the next step is to check flap deflection or travel. Doing so will require the use of the prop protractor, or the

On takeoff as well as landing, non-identical flap droop can affect the feel of a plane. To counter wing-heaviness, one can droop the affected wing's flap or bend a fixed tab. Some Mooney owners bend the appropriate aileron—a procedure requiring delicacy and familiarity with the manufacturer's recommendations. Extreme care should be taken.

substitute devices we have talked about. Level the aircraft about its roll axis, putting the carpenter's level across the seat rails or other suitable points recommended by the manufacturer, and letting air out of one or the other tire until leveling is accomplished. Then mark off points on each flap, next to a rib and equi-distant from the wing roots on each side of the airplane. Due to the nuances of geometry, the points you mark off don't need (strictly speaking) to be parallel to the aircraft centerline, but they should be close, and at equal angles. You can assure that the tape lines you establish are at similar angles by lining up pieces of 3/4-inch masking tape immediately adjacent to rib rivet lines. This gives surprisingly good accuracy.

Now extend the flaps one notch at a time and record the angular change on each side of the airplane. Any disparity from side to side as the flaps are extended will necessitate a close look by a mechanic, for either something is worn, or a bellcrank is not properly aligned. (The geometry of bellcranks, as you probably know, is such that the rate of displacement is not always linear. If one is improperly set and the up limits of the flap—or other control—were adjusted by changing the length of a pushrod, the down limits and neutral point could be substantially off.)

Once the flaps are trued out, you will have been exposed to the techniques used to rig the rest of the controls (with exceptions, of course, for certain specially designed control features on some airplanes—such as the all-moving-tail trim design on the Mooneys). Unlike flap rigging, the first step in rigging the flight controls is to lock the cockpit controls and bellcranks in their neutral position. Larger and more sophisticated aircraft rely upon *rigging pins* to accomplish this task; many of the planes we fly have no such provisions (although they may use a glorified clevis pin or bolt that slips through matching holes in bellcranks and associated bracketry). Thus, our service manuals often tell us to clamp or tape pieces of wood to the rudder pedals or across the yokes of dual-control aircraft, so that everything is neutralized. For the most part, this method is satisfactory, at least for ailerons.

Where rigging pins are not used, manufacturers sometimes resort to various special alignment marks or templates. For example, on the Comanche 180, the service manual includes a dimensional drawing of a template that an owner or shop can fabricate in order to make checks of the outboard aileron bellcranks. Alternatively, one can use linear dimensions, such as the distance of the yoke from the panel, in order to obtain elevator neutral. In nearly all cases, when attempting to neutralize the rudder pedals, aircraft with nosewheels need to have their nose tire elevated off the ground; taildraggers must likewise be blocked up to allow the tailwheel to swing freely.

Once the cabin controls—including the trim controls—are neutralized in accordance with service-manual recommendations, take a peek outside. Ideally the outboard tips of the ailerons will be lined up with the trailing edge of the wingtip fairings, the trim tabs will be in trail, and the rudder will be in neutral. And the nose wheel will face dead-ahead. The odds of finding such circumstances are nil, actually—even for new airplanes—unless the airframe has recently been tweaked by rigmasters.

Elevator Tips

The elevator rigging is set in a similar manner to the ailerons. Neutral on the yoke or stick, as far as fore/aft travel is concerned, is usually set dimensionally. To a large degree, this is a matter of comfort and convenience, although with a stick-controlled aircraft, a joystick that is rigged too far aft of neutral can sometimes rub on the seats at full aft travel.

If elevator cable tension is too loose, it is possible that the aircraft will not have adequate elevator control authority. One wonders how many Cessna 182s and 205s and early 206s have sustained firewall damage due to landing hard on the nosewheel solely because of low cable tension, which allows the yoke to be limited by the secondary stops, instead of the primaries? It makes sense to modify checklists to include a check of control-travel stops *before* starting the engine(s). In that manner, if you bang the stops *a bit*, you can hear if the controls hit their primary stops before being limited by the secondaries. (Try that trick while the engines are running.)

Rudder Travel

Rudder travel, tension, and limit stops are also set similar to the above. Rather than use the prop protractor, service manuals describe dimensional checks (usually) which correlate with desired deflection angles. In the case of our Comanche, the tailcone fairing is removed, and a piece of welding rod is taped into the trailing edge of the single-piece rudder skin, in the sharp radius (or fold) of that skin, where it was formed with a sheet-metal brake. The control-cable tension is set, tightening up each of the control cables until both cable tensions match, and the welding rod is centered over a centerline drawn—in accordance with the manual—on a piece of tape.

With the rudder centered and the pedals still secured, the next step (normally) is to rig the nosewheel to neutral. If your aircraft has a tendency to dart off the runway shortly after touchdown, it's usually just as the nosewheel touches down. (If your aircraft has a tailwheel and you notice the same tendency, don't be too alarmed.)

The rudder pedals are then freed, and the travel is also checked dimensionally, as a distance to either side of centerline. Control stops are again set so that the primary stops limit control travel first, just before meeting the secondaries.

Trim Systems

Trim systems are extremely diverse. Check your service manual. Generally, pitch trim systems use continuous cable loops with jackscrews or spools at the actuator end for mechanical advantage. In any case, control cable tensions are set with the tensiometer. It is important to ensure that jackscrews and other mechanisms are neutralized or at a specific setting when the control surface itself is neutralized. With electric-trim systems, there are also clutch breakaway settings to check, and your manual may give a specific time (in seconds) for the motor to go from one trim extreme to the opposite extreme with battery voltage and a given load applied to the trim surface. Consult your service manual, naturally, when there is any question of how to proceed.

Mooneys, Et Cetera

As for you lucky guys with Mooneys: Pushrod-actuated controls obviously do not require adjustments with tensiometers! In fact, once set at the factory, push-pull-tube controls should remain in pretty good rig until the ugly day comes when someone goofs and damages the airframe. Even so, it remains important to check limit stops and surface travels, as they can often be adjusted to make the airplane fly in better trim. The dimensional, protractor and limit stops checks are essentially the same as for any cable-actuated-controls airplane. Adjustment consists, for the most part, of screwing rod ends in or out—or replacing them altogether, if they've worn severely or frozen (corroded).

Odds are that once a rigging check is started, you will discover that your rudder cables are slapping around on the belly of the airplane, that loose cables don't give the elevator or stabilator its required authority, and/or that all controls are slightly out of whack. As you tighten up turnbuckles, you will be amazed at what two or three turns here, an eighth of an inch of slack taken out there, and a half-turn of a rod end, will do. Usually, with very little tweaking, everything falls into place.

A final word of caution: Before you get antsy and decide to go flying, be certain to check each and every turnbuckle for proper safetying. Remove all rigging pins, and make sure any hardware that was loosened or removed is replaced and tightened. Then, when you are done, go fly on a calm, cool morning. You will be astonished at how the doggiest airplane becomes a pleasure to fly.

CHECKING TRIM TAB FREE-PLAY

Most pilots are aware of the importance of elevator trim tab free play. In aircraft that have a trim tab, the tab acts in servo-fashion to apply pressure to (or move) the elevator—the tail wags the dog, so to speak. Obviously, in such a system it pays to keep free play to a minimum, since a trim tab that's free to flop back and forth can easily convince the elevator to do likewise, setting up perfect conditions for divergent flutter.

The question is, how much trim tab play is too much? And what can one do to correct it? Surprisingly, these issues are frequently not addressed at all in small-plane service manuals.

Most Cessna owners—and many mechanics—are not aware of the fact that the Cessna factory recommends that the trim tab actuator be removed from the aircraft (regardless of model) for inspection, lubrication, and adjustment (to remove play) every 1,000 hours *or three years*, whichever comes first. In addition, Cessna recommends that free play be measured every 100 hours of operation.

Free Play Inspection

If trim tab tolerances are not called out in your airplane's service

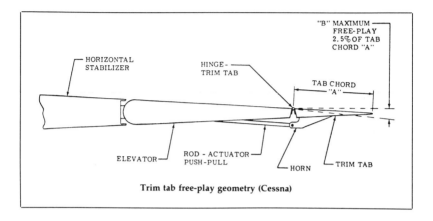

Trim tab free-play geometry (Cessna)

manual, the following free play inspection procedure—based on tolerances established in FAA AC43.13-1A (par. 55)—can be used:

1. Place elevators and trim tab(s) in a flush-neutral position.

2. Using no more than moderate pressure, move the trim tab trailing edge up and down by hand. Measure the total free play at the trailing edge with a ruler.

3. Determine whether observed free play is acceptable by comparing it to 2.5 percent of the tab chord (measured at hinge). If play is less than 2.5 percent of chord, the system is within prescribed limits. (Example: The maximum allowable free play for a tab measuring 4.0 inches in width would be 4.0 X .025, or .100 inch.)

If trim tab free play is greater than 2.5 percent of chord, check the following items (Cessna models):

—Inspect the push-pull tube to tab horn attachment for looseness while moving the tab up and down.

—Check the push-pull tube to actuator assembly rod-end attachment for looseness.

—Check for looseness of the rod end in the actuator assembly, with the push-pull tube disconnected.

When the source of sources of the excess play have been identified, repairs should be made either by replacing the affected components (rod ends, attach bolts, etc.) or by servicing the actuator, as needed.

Cessna Actuator Service

Cessna trim tab actuators should be removed from the aircraft and inspected every 1,000 hours or three years (see Cessna Service Letter SE73-25). The Cessna-recommended procedure is outlined below. Note: The following work can be done by the pilot under a mechanic's supervision, but the final logbook signoff must be by a licensed A&P. (Numbers refer to the accompanying diagram.)

First, be sure the airplane's tail is supported properly, to allow work in the tailcone.

After removing the baggage compartment aft bulkhead (to gain access to the trim system cables), remove safety wire from elevator trim turnbuckle, relieving system tension. Remove access cover(s) from rear of plane as needed to gain access to trim actuator and push-pull tube; then unbolt push-pull tube from actuator rod end (6).

Next, remove the chain guard (2), if applicable, and disengage chain from actuator sprocket (14). Then remove attach hardware

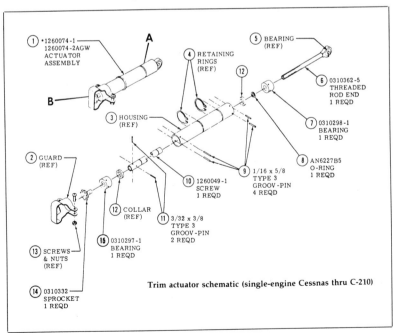

Trim actuator schematic (single-engine Cessnas thru C-210)

from actuator and carefully remove actuator from aircraft.

The actuator can be disassembled as follows:

1. Using punch and hammer, knock out Groov-Pins (11) securing sprocket (14) to screw shaft (10). Separate shaft from sprocket.

2. Unscrew threaded rod end (6), separating it from actuator.

3. Drive out Groov-Pins (9) securing bearings (7) in housing (3).

4. Lightly tap screw shaft (10) at sprocket end to remove bearing (7), O-ring (8), an collar (12).

5. Tap shaft (10) from opposite direction to remove bearing (15) and collar (12) at sprocket end.

Note: It is not necessary to remove retaining rings (4).

When the actuator has been disassembled as above, wash all parts *except the rod end bearing (5)* in Stoddard solvent or equivalent. Then inspect the parts for obvious damage (deep nicks, cracks, etc.), rejecting defective units. Inspect bearings (7, 15) and rod end (6) for excessive wear or scoring.

Acceptable dimensions are as follows:

Bearing (15) I.D.: .373 inch min., .380 inch max.

Bearing (7) I.D.: .248/.253 (small diameter), .373/.380 (large diameter).

Rod end (6) O.D., shank: .242/.246.

Screw shaft (10) O.D.: .367/.370 (at bearing surfaces).

Note: relative linear movement between internal threaded screw shaft (10) and bearing (7) should be .004 inch to .010 inch at room temperature.

Check all threads for damage, foreign particles that may impair smooth operation, etc. and reject obviously defective parts.

Check the sprocket (14) for broken, chipped, stepped or worn teeth.

Replace (don't repair) defective parts found during the above inspections.

Actuator Reassembly

Discard all Groov-Pins (9, 11) and O-rings (8). Lubricate collars (12), screw shaft (10), and threaded rod end (6) with MIL-G-21164C high and low temperature grease (molybdenum disulfide type grease). Then build up the actuator as follows:

First, install collar (12) and bearing (15) on screw shaft (10). Press sprocket (14) into end of screw shaft (10), align pin holes, and install new Groov-Pins (11).

Next, insert shaft (10) into housing (3), with housing oriented to sprocket end as it was during disassembly. Press bearing (15) into housing until flush with end.

If a new bearing (15) is to be installed, it must be final-drilled before assembly into housing. Use a 1/16-inch (.0625) drill bit and carefully orient the drill so that the bit will emerge through hole on opposite side of housing (3) without enlarging the existing hole. Then press bearing into place and drive new Groov-Pins into the 1/16-inch holes.

Now install collar (12), new O-ring (8), and bearing (7) on screw shaft (10) at opposite end of housing. Press bearing in until flush. (If new bearing is to be used, final-drill the Groov-Pin holes as outlined above.) Press Groov-Pins into holes.

If a new rod end bearing is required (5), press bearing into rod end boss, being sure the pressing force bears against the outer race of the bearing so as not to damage parts.

Finally, screw the threaded rod end (6) into shaft (10).

Operational Check

Before installing the newly serviced actuator on the aircraft, test it by rotating the sprocket (14) with your fingers while holding the rod end (6) stationary. The rod end should travel back and forth (in/out) smoothly, with no indication of binding.

Now reinstall the actuator by following the removal steps in reverse order; rig the trim system in accordance with your aircraft service manual; safety the turnbuckle(s); replace access covers; and recheck trim tab free play.

The intensive, comprehensive inspections we have discussed in this section are a vital lifeline between the pilot and his airplane. They provide a measure of security and peace-of-mind that any conscientious owner-pilot would welcome. Formidable though these procedures may seem to the uninitiated, they can become comfortably familiar. The more conscientious the regime of scrutiny and follow-through, the more such preventive maintenance (when legally performed) can save in money, work, and time.

As we have seen, these benefits extend through most of the other procedures we have discussed in this volume—perhaps even to the annual inspection, if it is performed in such a way and at such times that it truly sustains the integrity of the airplane.

Any owner welcomes the serenity and sense of security that comes with flying an essentially trouble-free airplane. It is to his advantage to develop the skills, the knowledge, and the confidence to contribute directly to the monitoring of his aircraft. To serve this enlightened self-interest and assist in the obtaining of helpful maintenance information has been the purpose of this sixth volume, as it is for the entire Light Plane Maintenance Library.

APPENDIX

Appendix

CONTROL SYSTEM
TROUBLESHOOTING

Note:The following information is presented for educational purposes only. FAR Part 43 specifies who may and may not perform maintenance on a U.S.-registered aircraft.

Ailerons

SYMPTOM	POSSIBLE CAUSE	REMEDY
Lost motion in control wheel	Word rod ends.	Check visually replace worn rod ends.
	Loose control cables.	Check and adjust cable tension
	Broken pulley.	Check visually; replace broken parts.
	Sprung bellcranks.	Check visually; replace defective parts.
	Loose chains.	Adjust chain tension.

Ailerons (continued)

SYMPTOM	POSSIBLE CAUSE	REMEDY
Resistance to control wheel movement.	Cables too tight.	Adjust cable tension.
	Pulleys binding.	Observe pulleys as ailersons are operated. If binding, replace pulley.
	Rusted chain.	Check chain behind panel. Replace if rusted.
	Cable jumped pulley.	Replace cable on pulley.
	Defective U-joints, if used.tive parts.	Replace defec-
Control wheel not level with ailerons neutral.	Improper adjustment of chains or cables.	Adjust rigging per aircraft manual.
Dual control wheels not coordinated.	Chain not properly adjusted on sprockets.	Adjust chain rigging.

Elevators

SYMPTOM	POSSIBLE CAUSE	REMEDY
Binding or jerky motion in elevator control.	Cables slack.	Adjust cable tension.
	Defective elevator hinges.	Move elevator by hand to check hinges. Replace defective parts.
	Defective 'T', 'Y', or 'U' pivot bearings.	Disconnect parts and check pivots for free movement. Replace defective parts.
	Cables not riding on on pulleys correctly.	Check/correct cable routing.
	Clevis bolts too tight.	Adjust to eliminate bolt binding.
	Defective control column needle bearing rollers.	Replace defective rollers.

Elevators (continued)

SYMPTOM	POSSIBLE CAUSE	REMEDY
Elevator fails to attain prescribed travel.	Cables unevenly tightened.	Rig per aircraft manual.
	Stops incorrectly set.	Rig per aircraft manual.

Rudder

SYMPTOM	POSSIBLE CAUSE	REMEDY
Binding or jerky movement of rudder pedals.	Rudder is hitting tail cone.	Readjust tail cone.
	Cables too tight, cables cables misrouted, binding or defective pulleys or cable guards, etc.	Adjust cable tension, route cables properly, replace defective parts.
	Pedal bars require lubrication.	Apply general-purpose oil to pivot points.

Rudder (continued)

SYMPTOM	POSSIBLE CAUSE	REMEDY
Binding or jerky movement of rudder pedals.	Defective rudder hinge bushings or bearings, or bellcrank bearings.	Replace defective parts.
	Steering rods not properly adjusted.	Adjust per aircraft manual.
Incorrect rudder travel.	Bent push-pull rods (if used).	Replace bent parts.
	Incorrect rigging.	Rig per aircraft manual specs.
Lost motion between pedals and rudder.	Insufficient cable tension.	Adjust cable tension.

INDEX

Index